$uperthief

A Master Burglar,

the Mafia,

and the

Biggest Bank Heist in U. S. History

$UPERTHIEF

Rick Porrello

Copyright © 2006 Rick Porrello

Published by Next Hat Press
P.O. Box 23
Novelty, OH 44072
Superthief.com

Subsidiary Rights Manager:
Peter Miller, President
PMA Literary & Film Management, Inc.
212-929-1222
E-mail: pmalitfilm@aol.com
Website: www.pmalitfilm.com

Printed and Distributed by BookMasters, Inc.
Sales: 800-247-6553, Fax: 419-281-6883
Bookmasters.com

Interior Design: Jonathan Gullery
Cover Design: Jonathan Gullery and Rick Porrello
Editor: Laurie Viera Rigler

ISBN: 0-9662508-5-0
ISBN-13: 978-0-9662508-5-5

Library of Congress Control Number: 2005927465

Cataloging-in-Publication Data
Porrello, Rick.
Superthief : a master burglar, the mafia, and the biggest bank heist in U. S. history /
Rick Porrello.
p.   cm.

1. Christopher, Phil, 1943- . 2. Bank robberies—California—Laguna Niguel. 3. Bank Robberies—Ohio—Lordstown. 4. Burglary—California. 5. Mafia—Ohio. 6. Thieves-Ohio—Cleveland—Biography. I. Title.
HV6653.C47 P67 2005
364.1552092—dc22 2005927465

First Printing

Other Books by the Author

To Kill the Irishman – the War that Crippled the Mafia
The story of notorious Mafia foe Danny Greene.
Under option for a motion picture.

The Rise and Fall of the Cleveland Mafia – Corn Sugar and Blood
Mafia boss-turned cooperating witness Angelo "Big Ange"
Lonardo and the Porrello-Lonardo sugar war.

Renaissance man Rick Porrello—a former drummer for Sammy Davis Jr, a veteran cop, and the current webmaster of a respected anti-Mafia website—presents an exquisitely vivid anatomy of the largest bank burglary in U.S. history. Well-written and fast-paced, Superthief, is a remarkable insider's view of how this complex crime was planned and executed. Rich with heart-pounding immediacy throughout the plot, it is Porrello's finest work to date."

Dan E. Moldea, author of *The Hoffa Wars*

Rick Porrello masterfully takes us into the intricate workings of the mind of a thief. Your heart will pulsate with each page turned as if you were pulling the heist yourself. Best of all the author illustrates the redeeming quality of this book—the message that Crime Does Not Pay.

Georgia Durante, author of *The Company She Keeps*

Superthief is an entertaining and sometimes humorous view into the mob-connected life of a master burglar. With Rick Porrello's sharp writing and crisp dialogue, Superthief reads like a Hollywood screenplay. It's a truly worthwhile addition to anyone's true-crime collection.

Scott M. Deitche, author, *Cigar City Mafia:*
A Complete History of the Tampa Underworld

Superthief is the best insider's view of the criminal life since Pileggi's Wiseguy. Author Rick Porrello takes the reader on a riveting journey into the work-a-day life of a professional thief, through burglaries, jewelry heists and culminating with the Big Job. Entertaining and enlightening, this book is a MUST READ for anyone with an interest in American-style criminal justice.

T. J. English, author of *The Westies and Paddy Whacked*

To Christian and Camille, my super kids

Author's Note and Acknowledgments

Because of my work as a crime author and host of *AmericanMafia.com*, I have been contacted numerous times by organized crime figures searching for a writer to coauthor their stories. While some of the stories have sounded promising, I've opted to stick with my own comfortably paced literary agenda. As a career cop and jazz drummer, I only have time for one writing project at a time.

Things changed in 2000, when I received an intriguing letter from Mary Ann Kowalski, the future Mrs. Phil Christopher. I already knew of Phil, a burglar and organized crime associate, and had heard he was writing a book about his life. But I was unfamiliar with the details of the United California Bank burglary he had been involved in. After viewing a fascinating segment about the crime in a Discovery Channel documentary about infamous burglaries and robberies, I asked Mary Ann for more material. She provided me with Phil's rough manuscript. All twelve hundred, handwritten pages. It was titled *Superthief*.

Writing professionals will look at nothing unless it is neatly typed and presented in a concise and coherent format according to industry protocol. But I found *Superthief* so promising that I overlooked the rough writing and poor organization and delved in. I could not put the manuscript down. Hidden in those twelve hundred pages, I saw a compelling and honest tale of a professional criminal's life on the streets, his betrayal by friends, his life in prison, the tragic endings for his friends, and the firsthand account of a crime that made history. I also saw significant theatrical potential and knew I had been brought a winner.

I immediately reworked my projected writing schedule and signed a collaboration agreement with Mary Ann. Thus began almost five years of research, writing, and revision.

Out of respect for their privacy, I decided to change the names of Phil's former girlfriends and ex-wives. Additionally, I have altered several details concerning one of them to further protect her identity. The fictitious names are Sandy, Maggie, Diane, and Anna. Anna is a composite character based on two of the women.

In order to avoid confusing a primary player in the United California Bank burglary with a secondary figure who had the same first name, I gave the secondary figure the fictitious name of Billy.

At the time of this writing, the central figure in this book, Phil Christopher, is still in prison. Consequently, access to him has been my biggest challenge in writing this book. I corresponded with Phil primarily by letter, but on occasion we spoke by phone, and I was able to interview him in person several times in federal prisons in Pennsylvania and Ohio. Due to prison regulations, none of the interviews I conducted for this book were tape recorded. In most cases, I recreated dialogue based on Phil's manuscript, my letters, conversations, and interviews with him, and my phone interviews with other sources.

Mary Ann Christopher has been a cordial, professional, and patient collaborator to work with. I thank her for entrusting me with this project.

I would like to publicly express my gratitude to my editor, Laurie Viera Rigler, whose critical eye, dedication, and unwavering encouragement have been invaluable to this book, and to my writing career.

And of course, I would like to thank *Superthief* himself, Phil Christopher, for his cooperation and candor in documenting his story.

Rick Porrello
September, 2005

$uperthief

Chapter One

On the afternoon of August 17, 2003, Phil Christopher was seated in a common area of the Cuyahoga County Jail in his hometown of Cleveland, Ohio. He had been transported there from Loretto Federal Correctional Institution in Pennsylvania, where he was serving his fourth year of a ten-year sentence for conspiracy to traffic in drugs.

Phil was no stranger to courtrooms. But this appearance would be different. This time he wasn't a defendant; he had been subpoenaed as a witness in a murder investigation—a murder that had taken place in 1968.

This wasn't the first time that the 1968 murder of pimp Andrew "Arnie" Prunella had come back to haunt Phil Christopher. Late in 1982, Phil, along with Owen and Martin Kilbane, had been indicted for the murder. But in early 1983, Phil had his case severed from the Kilbanes, and accepted a plea bargain in which he pled guilty to a reduced charge of voluntary manslaughter. Part of the agreement was that Phil would not be required to testify against the Kilbanes at their trial.

But twenty-one years later, the case was reopened, and the Kilbanes were under investigation by a grand jury. Phil's obligations were now uncertain. While his 1983 plea agreement stated that he could not be compelled to testify against the Kilbanes in that trial, it did not address the possibility of a future grand jury investigation. Refusing to answer questions could very well bring a contempt of court charge—and more prison time.

Phil waited for the case to move forward. And in the meantime, his wife, Mary Ann, could visit him in the Cuyahoga County Jail without making the four-hour drive to Loretto. When Mary Ann wasn't there, Phil passed the time by exercising, reading, and playing cards. On that particular afternoon of August 17, 2003, Phil was sitting at a white steel bench and table, studying the five cards in his right hand, when his concentration was broken.

PHIL: I heard a corrections officer call out my name. I told the inmate I was playing cards with that I'd be back soon. I laid my cards face down, got up, and walked over to the door separating the lounge from the main corridor. The guard on the other side motioned in a circle with his finger. I turned my back to the door, clasped my hands together, and put them through the opening. He handcuffed me, opened the door, and escorted me down the corridor.

I asked where we were going, and the guard reminded me that I had asked to go to confession. My heart started pounding. He brought me to an eight-foot by ten-foot visiting room, took the handcuffs off, and left. The heavy metal door thundered shut, and I sank down on one of two benches that were bolted to the wall. My mind was racing with images of sins I had committed, flashing through my head like an out-of-control movie projector. My hand on the steering wheel of the boat, then the stars. The steering wheel. The stars.

I wondered if I'd made a stupid mistake. There were some things I wanted to confess that I'd never got caught for. I checked under the benches, then stepped up and inspected the vents. I heard the lock clank open, and Father Dismas walked in. We shook hands as the guard closed the door. Father Dismas gestured toward the benches, and we sat down facing each other. I told him I was very nervous about this, and I asked if the room was bugged. He laughed and said it wasn't. I told him I wanted to do the right thing by going to confession. It had been many years, and I said I didn't know where to start. He suggested I simply start from the beginning.

I told Father Dismas about the first time I got in trouble stealing. I was nine years old. The milkman came once a week to collect payments. On the hottest days of summer, I used to sneak into his truck and take a piece of ice. But one day I saw the door to the front of the truck unlocked. I opened it and found a big leather pouch with lots of change in it.

Before the milkman returned, I took the pouch, ran from the truck, and hid under my front porch to make sure nobody saw me. I buried the bag of coins there. Two days later when I brought it out, my mother caught me. She asked me where I got it, and I told her I found it by the street. She figured it out, though. I thought I'd be in big trouble, but my mother never told my father. She just gave the money back, telling the milkman that my little brother, who was only five years old, had found it on the street.

Once I started talking to Father Dismas, I was more at ease. But I had a feeling he knew there were more serious things on my mind. He listened patiently as I told him about a childhood friend of mine who was an altar boy. My friend used to help count the money from Sunday mass collection. But he would also help himself to one hundred or two hundred dollars a week. He was scared to keep the money at home, so I hid it for him and he gave me an equal share. At one point I had almost one thousand dollars in my bedroom closet, but my parents never caught me. I was ashamed to tell Father Dismas that one, but he just nodded every few seconds.

Finally I got to Arnie Prunella. I wondered how I'd get through that.

Chapter Two

Things could have turned out differently for Philip Christopher, who was born in 1943 into a hard-working, law-abiding family who lived in the Collinwood district of Cleveland, Ohio.

It was an era when nobody locked their doors.

Unlike most Italian-American families of that generation, Philip's immediate family was small. He, his parents, and younger brother lived on Alhambra Street in a modest, two-story house with a front porch, and just a quarter mile from the railroad tracks. A city bus mechanic, Philip's father, Joseph, was a first-generation Italian-American whose surname, before it was Americanized, was Cristofaro. Like many of the Italian men in Collinwood, Joseph Christopher made wine in his spare time and enjoyed opera recordings, which were played on Victrolas. Philip's mother, Irene, was a quiet, unassuming first-generation German-American who kept a traditional Italian home.

Italian culture was a celebrated part of life in Collinwood. Old Italian women could be seen each morning either walking to mass or the produce market—some of them skillfully balancing baskets of fruits and vegetables on their heads. In the fall when backyard gardens were being harvested, the fragrance of stewing tomatoes drifted through Collinwood's side streets, with almost every lady of the house busily canning for the winter.

The Catholic religion was no less a Collinwood virtue than the Italian culture, with three Catholic churches serving the area. Philip's mother and father did not attend mass but often sent Philip, along with a donation, to Holy Redeemer Church. Philip would merely drop off the envelope, then continue on his way to meet his friends.

On weekdays and Saturdays, roving street merchants traveled the streets of Collinwood by truck, selling fruit, vegetables, and other necessities. One old Italian huckster still used a horse and wagon to pick up unwanted newspapers and clothing. "Pape-a-Raigs! Pape-a-Raigs!" he shouted, hawking his papers and rags. Another familiar sound was the clanging bell of the baker as he drove through the neighborhood. When residents waved to him from their doors, he would pull over and present a tray of fresh and still-warm bread and goodies to choose from. And there was Ruby the ice cream man, who also sold fireworks in July, when it seemed every family had an amateur pyrotechnician.

The highlight of summer life in Collinwood was the Holy Redeemer Church Feast of the Assumption, the August 15 Catholic holiday celebrating the Virgin Mary's departure from earthly life and assumption of her body and soul into heaven. The "feast," as it was better known, was marked by a procession in honor of the Virgin. It featured a life-size statue of Mary, cloaked with hundreds of dollar bills—donations to the church. The statue would be followed by a brass band and devout widowed women, dressed in black, carrying rosaries, and singing in Italian. The communion class of formally dressed boys and girls in white would follow, all walking solemnly through the streets, preceded by two mounted policemen.

For Philip and his friends, the feast meant three days of fun and food. There were pony rides and games of skill, like the greased telephone pole. Whoever could manage the slippery climb to the flag at the top won a prize. A fireworks display capped the last night.

During the feast, the streets were jammed with parked cars and revelers pressing toward the mouthwatering aromas of steaming pasta, pizza, and fried dough. For the adults, there was beer and various games of chance like Chuck-a-Luck, in which bets were placed on the outcome of three dice tumbled in a spinning cage. For Philip and his friends, there was the hunt for dropped coins, which capped off the end of each feast night.

Philip Christopher was a typically energetic, active boy who spent much of his time exploring the residential and industrial district that was Collinwood, which was bounded by Lake Erie to the north and divided in half by railroad tracks. He and his friends would hike along the New York Central railroad tracks, hunting garden snakes and pollywogs, or tadpoles. Bored with that, they'd climb to the top of a stopped train, run along several cars, and then jump to the ground.

When not running through the neighborhood, Philip was playing sports, his childhood love. An excellent athlete, his favorite game was baseball. He pitched for the Holy Redeemer team, which practiced on a diamond behind the church, and he played on all of the Little League teams and won trophies. He also won medals for his skill in swimming and archery, which he learned at the local YMCA.

PHIL: As a boy, I was ambitious and goal-oriented, and always strived to do my best at everything. I always wanted to go camping at the YMCA with the rest of the kids, but my parents couldn't afford the fee. One year you could sell candy and put it toward the price of camp. And so I went door to door and sold my entire way to camp. Another time I wanted a camera. The school had a fundraiser where you had to sell sachet that women put in their dressers to make their clothes smell nice. The prize was a camera. I sold enough and got the camera. When I was eleven, I had a Cleveland Press newspaper route. I made four cents profit on each newspaper, plus tips. I made about fifty dollars on my first Christmas. But my route didn't last long.

I was twelve years old and had just started at Collinwood Junior High School when I got an earache that wouldn't go away. Then I started getting bloody noses for no reason. My mother took me to the doctor, who put me in the hospital. I got so sick I couldn't get out of bed. I was often in pain, with swelling on the side of my head, my eyes, knees, and feet. After a few days, I was diagnosed with rheumatic fever.

When my father's mother heard that kids used to die of rheumatic fever, she started visiting me every day. My grandmother would sit there, holding her rosary and saying prayers to herself.

After two weeks in the hospital, I was allowed to go home. I couldn't walk upstairs, so my mother and father brought my bed downstairs. I slept in the dining room all summer, and every week the doctor would come to the house to check on me. The time went by very slowly, but my parents did what they could, like buying me three-foot-long model boats to build. There was an ocean liner and a sailboat named Sea Witch. I even watched soap operas. My mother would ask me about the episode, and I would fill her in.

I was put on a new drug called cortisone, which helped with the swelling and pain but caused me to gain weight. My friends would come over every day, and I was embarrassed because I had blown up like a balloon and gained thirty pounds. But I liked the company, and they would update me on the highlights of the recent sports games at school.

After a couple of months, I was able to get out of bed and go out on the front porch. Since I was limited as to the amount of time I could stand on my feet, my friends pitched in and rented a wheelchair so I could go with them to the Holy Redeemer feast and a baseball game. It was the best time I'd had in months. I couldn't wait to get better so I could start playing sports again.

A week before summer vacation was over, the doctor said I could walk a little each day. I still remember the first day I walked down to the end of the street by myself. I was so tired I had to sit down on the sidewalk and rest before I went back.

It took quite a while to get my strength back. I slowly lost most of the weight and was feeling a lot better. Soon the doctor said I was as good as new and would even be able to play sports again. But in order to play sports in high school, your parents had to sign a form, a liability waiver, in case you got hurt. I couldn't believe it, but my father wouldn't sign the form. He wouldn't let me play, insisting that it was for my own good. He was worried because I had been so sick. So that was the end of my sports that I loved playing.

It was during this time that I started to notice that some kids were better off financially than I was. I had a comfortable home, but I wanted the things that kids from wealthier families had. I saw kids go to school and buy their lunch, while I brought a bag lunch. I saw that some boys got trousers made at the neighborhood tailor, while I got hand-me-down clothes from my cousin. Some of the older kids would even get a nice car from their parents. I wanted extra money, too, so I could have some of these nice things.

I had only stolen once before, when I was nine. But now with more time on my hands since I wasn't playing sports, stealing was becoming a habit I couldn't break. It was a thrill to steal something without getting caught. When we wanted something and didn't have any money, we would just take it. We'd travel on our bikes, and the other kids would keep the clerk busy at the counter while I stole Popsicles, candy, or pop—whatever we wanted that day. When the huckster would come around, one of my friends would keep him busy while I was on the other side of the truck stealing fruit. I was the one who always took the risk because the other kids were scared.

This was around the time when I was hiding money for my friend who worked at the church every Sunday, counting and stealing from the collections. He and I started hanging around this store and got to be friendly with the girl who worked there. We'd go behind the counter to help her out, but we also helped ourselves to money from the cash register. A few weeks later, we took too much at one time. The shop owner figured out we were stealing and told us we weren't allowed in his store anymore.

One time when I was fourteen, another friend and I had just left a party. We were walking down the street looking in car windows for something to steal. One car had the keys in it. I knew a little about driving, so we got in and I took off. I drove back to the party, picked up a bunch of the guys, and went for a joyride.

After a while we decided to head back. I pulled into a field to turn around, and the car got stuck in the dirt. While we were trying to get the car out, the police came and we all ran. I got away, but somebody who got caught told on me. The police came to my house and took me to the detention home. I got out a day later, went to court, and was put on probation for six months. To make matters worse, the church workers finally noticed money missing, and my friend couldn't help with the collections anymore. That was the end of a lot of easy cash. It was terrible not having money when it had been so plentiful for so long.

I stayed out of trouble for a few months while I was on probation, but when I was fifteen, my friends and I started going "hoopin" which was breaking into car trunks to steal tires. We would get ten dollars for each new tire. We also made good money stealing hubcaps and wheel skirts.

I was very free with the money I stole and would always treat the kids in the neighborhood to pop or ice cream. At Euclid Beach, an amusement park by Lake Erie, I paid for all of my friends' rides. We'd go to the municipal baseball stadium and watch the Indians play, and I'd pay for the tickets and food. I even bought new bats and balls for our neighborhood baseball team.

I remember this big dance we wanted to go to at the Continental Ballroom, which was some distance from Collinwood. I got two cabs and paid for them to take us. Naturally I became very popular. My friends nicknamed me "MB," which stood for money bags.

There were a lot of thieves who lived in Collinwood. I don't mean pickpockets or shoplifters, but professional burglars—some of the best in the country. They could beat every alarm system and open any safe made. As kids, we looked up to them because of all the money they had. When I was sixteen, I hung around the basement of the dry cleaners, where they played cards, and behind the Grotto Inn by the boxing gym where they shot craps. They paid me to open the door and watch for the law. But the money wasn't enough for me. I wanted big money like they had.

I had real jobs, too. During the summer I would get up early to go to work at a country club. But most of the time, I would just hang out in Collinwood or go stealing. Then I would go home and make it look like I had been caddying. One summer day I had eighty dollars that I'd made on tires the night before. My brother didn't have a bicycle, and the neighborhood kids wouldn't let him play with theirs. So I went to the Western Auto Store and bought him a Schwinn bike, which cost me $79.99. I can still remember because they gave me a penny back. When my parents asked where I got the money, I told them it was from caddying.

Hanging around the older guys in the neighborhood paid off. They taught me different things and gave me tools to help me steal. Eugene Ciasullo, an up-and-coming Mafia enforcer, gave me two sets of master keys for all cars and trucks. After that, when I went hoopin' with my friends, we'd steal a truck to use.

One morning around 6:00 a.m., when I was supposed to be at the country club, a couple of friends and I stole a truck from a potato chip company to haul our stolen tires. I looked in the back, and it was loaded with bags of potato chips and pretzels. We had to get rid of them to make room for the tires, so I told my friend, who was driving, to go slowly through the neighborhood. Then I started tossing out boxes of chips and pretzels. I told him the younger kids would have a ball on their way to school.

Another time we had stolen a truck to transport a load of televisions that were in a boxcar at the Collinwood railroad yard. We knew someone who worked there, and he always told us when there were good loads to steal.

I was inside the boxcar handing televisions to two guys on the ground, when all of a sudden the train started moving. One of the guys got into the truck and started driving slowly while I kept handing the TVs down to the other guy, who kept running alongside the train and putting them in the truck. When the train started moving too fast, I jumped off.

It was around this time that I learned how to break into a safe. Eugene, who gave me the master keys to steal trucks, taught me a simple way. It was called "peeling." You had to use a steel wedge and sledgehammer, and I got very good at it.

I was sixteen when I planned my first score involving a safe. A buddy named Allie Calabrese and I got a couple of other kids from Collinwood and broke into a drugstore that Eugene had picked out for us. First the four of us climbed to the top of the store, and I cut a hole in the roof. Then the other two kids wrapped a rope around the chimney and pulled on one end while we lowered ourselves down. Inside the drugstore, Allie and I found the safe and peeled it open like Eugene had taught us. We took all of the money in the safe and were ready to leave.

We called up to the other two kids with the rope, but there was no answer. So we pulled on the rope, but it fell in. Allie started to panic, and I had to calm him down. I had him help me drag some filing cabinets under the hole, and we climbed up and out to find our two friends gone. We climbed down to the ground and called to them, and they answered from where they were hiding in some bushes. We asked what they were doing, and they said the cops had showed up and were parked outside the building. They said they'd yelled to us, but we never heard them.

We all left and went to count our money and split it up. Eugene got a share for picking out the store. I made sixteen hundred dollars that night on my first safe job. Needless to say, I was on my way. I thought I was the best.

Chapter Three

In 1962, Phil graduated from Collinwood High School with a C average. With his formal schooling out of the way, he continued his education on the streets, gravitating toward a well-established ring of skilled burglars, safecrackers, alarm men, and fences. His classrooms were Collinwood restaurants and taverns like Mirabiles and the Pointview Bar and Grill, which was the most popular bar in the neighborhood. The Pointview was not only the place to cash a paycheck, eat good Italian food, and have a drink to celebrate the end of the work week. It was also the unofficial headquarters for the best burglars in the region.

PHIL: These guys took a liking to me because I was ambitious, eager to learn, and a good listener. And so it wasn't long before they wanted me to have money and let me be the driver on some of their scores.

But around that time, I got another offer—a job with the Iron Workers Local 17 through a guy I met named Al Walsh, who was close with the bosses. He was ten years older, but we became good friends. He asked if I wanted to work with the union because it was election time and a young crew of members was trying to take control. Al said he needed more muscle—another guy who could be trusted—to protect Tom McDonald, the head business agent, and Walter Moore, a business agent who gave out the jobs from the union hall. Al also said the money was good, so naturally I said yes. It was better than being the driver on the occasional score.

Al was a gentleman but wasn't afraid of anything. I had no reputation at the time, except that I was with Al and stood my ground. I started by attending the pre-election meetings because the opposition would come in drunk and cause trouble. We carried guns because Paul Lyons, one of the main instigators, always had a piece on him. Paul was an iron worker with two personalities, one when he was drunk and one when he was sober. He was a real Jekyll and Hyde.

Nothing much happened at the meetings, except that the younger group would get mouthy. In the end the older regime won the election and retained control. There was a lot of work and everyone was making money. Things would be quiet until work got scarce, then the trouble would start again. The younger regime threatened Walter Moore, but we'd always be there to back him up.

At one point there was an election for business agent in Akron, just south of Cleveland. We were pushing to get one of our guys, Walter Hulka, elected so that we would have a representative there. After Walter won the election, Bob Cooney, the international vice president of the Iron Workers, called me to meet with him and gave me the task of accompanying Walter on his first day. I thought I was being tested because I was the only guy who was going to be with Walter. Bob gave me fifteen hundred dollars in cash and told me to be careful.

On Walter's first day, I drove to Akron and arrived at the union hall about a half hour before Walter was to arrive. There were already twenty or thirty guys there waiting for the jobs to be given out. I had a gun in the car with me but was debating bringing it in. Finally I decided that there were too many guys. If they started trouble, I couldn't shoot them all.

Walter pulled in, and I got out with him. As I walked toward the union hall, the guys outside stared at me. I just looked back and kept my head up as

I followed Walter inside. When I closed his office door behind us, I asked him if he'd seen any of the troublemakers outside.

"There's a few out there, but I don't think they'll cause any problems."

"I hope not," I said. "I'm the only one up here and I left my piece in the car."

Then we went outside, and Walter got ready to call the jobs off. One of the guys started walking toward Walter, and I stepped up to him. He was a big guy—a foot taller than I was and sixty or seventy pounds heavier. We locked glances for two or three seconds, then he offered his hand.

"I'm Frank."

"Phil Christopher."

He had a tight grip on my hand, and I squeezed back. I think he realized I wasn't a trembler.

"Nice to meet you, Phil," he said. Then he turned around and walked away.

That was the only time I thought there might be trouble. I stayed near Walter while he called the jobs off, then hung around the hall while he worked in his office. At the end of the day, I asked him what he wanted me to do. He said it didn't look like there would be any trouble, so I wouldn't have to come back the next day.

As a benefit of protecting the union bosses, I got my membership without having to do an apprenticeship. But I did learn to cut steel with an acetylene torch and was given choice construction jobs, mostly big high-rises where I learned to walk on newly placed steel beams.

Sandy, an Italian redhead I'd been going steady with since my first year of high school, was happy I had a good job. But she wanted to get married, and I wasn't ready. So we broke up and I started seeing other girls. After work I would head for the bars and have my fill of booze and broads. I paid cash for a car and had money in the bank, but I was spending a lot, too. I was having the time of my life.

A few months after Sandy and I broke up, I ran into her. She started crying, I felt bad, and we wound up getting back together. Not long after, we decided to get married. It was 1964, and I was doing well with the Iron Workers.

Sandy and I had a big wedding and went to Florida for our honeymoon. Then we moved into the bottom half of a double house. Our son, my only child, was born a year later.

Around that time, I went in partners with Al Walsh and two other guys on a bar—the Redwood Lounge in Collinwood. It was just an investment for Al and me because we were still working with the Iron Workers. The Redwood was a simple beer and wine bar, but my partners and I fancied it up. We paneled the walls and put in a dropped ceiling. We installed new soft, pink lighting that made everybody look good. It was so dim that your eyes had to adjust when you came in before you could see who was there. There were about twelve wooden stools with red padded seats and backs. On the opposite side of the bar was a long, red padded bench that ran the whole length of the wall. The tables were small with white tops and red padded chairs, and we put in a small dance floor in the back. We turned it into a fairly plush lounge, considering the neighborhood bar it had been. It was nice to have my own place to drink and entertain in.

Things were going well until work at the Iron Workers started getting scarce and the trouble started again. One day I was working as a union steward and had to go to the union hall to pay the work dues for the guys on my job. While I was there, Paul Lyons came in with a few guys. He was drunk. Walter Moore got nervous and asked me to get rid of him, so I went into the hallway where Paul was. I could see a bulge under his shirt. The other guys he was with didn't look like they had guns.

I went up to Paul and said, "How ya doing?"

"Fuck you, dago bastard," he said.

I got right in close in case he tried to go for his gun. The other guys were all looking at me, but I didn't take my eyes off Paul. He took a step back because I was right in his face. Then he reached for his gun. I grabbed at his arms with both hands real fast and got the gun away from him, then gave him a backhand slap.

"Now get the fuck out of here," I told them all, "before you find yourselves in pine boxes."

Fortunately they headed for the door because I had nobody backing me up.

As Paul was driving off in his big Lincoln, he yelled out the window, "I'm gonna kill you, dago mother-fucker!"

I kept hearing stories that Paul was out to get me. Guys I worked jobs with and who lived on the West Side would hear Paul making threats against me in bars. But I wasn't worried. I'd learned not to be afraid of a barking dog. But beware of the quiet one.

Not long after, I was in the Redwood when I heard a loud noise outside. Some black guy who worked at the tire company next door came running in and told me my car had been blown up. I had a 1965 Chevy Impala, and it was totaled by the bomb blast. I figured it was the younger regime.

About a week later, I got home late and saw two guys in my garage. I pretended like I didn't see them and went in the house and got my M1 carbine. As I walked toward the garage, which was about one hundred fifty feet from the house, they shot at me. I ducked behind a big tree and opened fire on them. We exchanged gunfire for about thirty seconds. Then they took off running and escaped over a fence. I went to check out the garage and found they had the hood up on my other car. I figured that Paul Lyons and his crew had been about to plant some dynamite.

A bunch of police cars came; then all the neighbors were standing outside their houses wondering what happened. I told the police officers that someone was trying to steal my car so I shot at him. They looked around, questioned me a little, then left.

At that point I knew I had to move my family because Paul Lyons was known to drive by people's houses and shoot through their front windows. I told Sandy we had to find another place to live because I was scared for her and our son, who was still a baby. It happened that a cousin of hers had a brick home in the neighborhood, and the upstairs was for rent. So I moved my family there right away and installed a big spotlight in the backyard.

Construction work was scarce now, and I started noticing old friends of mine who, like me, used to steal a lot as kids. But unlike me, they continued as adults. And unlike me, they were making good money and weren't tied down by regular jobs. So I went on a few scores with them and began making some fast money.

One of those guys, Charlie Broeckel, became my best friend after I helped him get away from the cops when he got hurt. I was driving the getaway car when a score we were on went bad. Charlie was on the roof of a three-story office building when the cops came in from the front. He jumped off the roof in the back. I could hear sirens, but I knew he was hiding somewhere in the area. So I drove around the block, came down a side street, and found Charlie hiding next to a garage. He had fractured both of his heels when he hit the ground. He sure was glad to see me.

Not long after I started stealing again, I realized that to make big money as a burglar, I had to know how to beat security systems. And so I started seeking out experts. There was this one kid named John from the neighborhood, who was very good with electronics. John sold marijuana and did some small-time burglaries when he needed money. He lived in the Coventry Road area in Cleveland Heights, which was all hippies back then, John included. Sometimes when I would stop over to talk about alarms, several of his friends would be there, kicking back, smoking dope, and listening to music. John taught me basic electronics—things like voltage, wattage, amperage, and Ohm's Law. He also made me my first alarm jumping box, which is used to defeat security systems electronically.

It seemed that the best burglars I was meeting were either from Collinwood or the Youngstown area. Most of the Youngstown guys were connected to crews who worked for either the Cleveland or Pittsburgh Mafia families. I was much younger than them, but they respected me because I was getting the reputation of being a solid guy—someone who could be trusted.

As I educated myself about being a burglar, I always sought out a lot of different teachers so that I could be sure I was doing things the best way. One of my first safe teachers was a guy named Dominic Senzarino. He was from Youngstown and better known as Junior. He had what he called a jig, which was made to bolt on to the safe door so you could drill easily. Junior introduced me to Skinny Sam Fossesca, a very skilled Youngstown burglar.

Skinny Sam was six feet tall and thin and five years older than me. He was bald on top and grew his hair real long on the sides so that he could comb it over the top of his head. He was also one of the best alarm jumpers in the country. He showed me more about the equipment I needed. Volt meters, batteries, probes and clips and line phones.

When I was comfortable with the basics of defeating burglar alarms, I decided to give myself some practical experience. I had a friend who owned a private club on St. Clair Avenue in Collinwood. He had an extra room in the back of the building where he stored stools, showcases, and other bar equipment. I asked him if I could use it because I was going to get this certain alarm installed to learned how it worked. I told him I would only need it for a couple of months. He was a close friend of my father, so I asked him not to say anything to him. He said okay but told me not to get into any trouble.

I called ADT Alarm Company, gave them a phony name, and told them I was starting a vending business. They sent a guy out who explained what kind of protection they had. I already knew most of it but played dumb. The system I picked was connected directly to the ADT central station. A few weeks later, they installed the alarm. It was a perfect set-up to learn—my own burglar school. If I made a mistake and the police came, I would simply say I was the business owner and had accidentally set it off. For the next few weeks, I experimented with the alarm system and practiced jumping it out. Finally I was confident that I could make some big money.

While I was with the Iron Workers and getting established as a burglar, I had the Redwood as my personal playground. I spent a lot of time there entertaining patrons, especially women. The Redwood became very popular, and my partners and I were always trying to make it better.

We had a dance floor and live music, but that didn't go too well, because it cost us more money for the band than we were taking in at the bar. Then we tried go-go girls for a while. But that didn't bring in too many guys to spend their money. Then I built a restaurant in the basement. That went pretty well.

I was a 26-year-old burglar and bar owner, and enjoying life in the fast lane. Money was king. That was my motto. At the Redwood we used to say, "Live fast, die young, and make a good-looking corpse." As for my marriage, it was dying young. I was young and wild, chasing broads all over, partying and buying rounds of drinks. Sometimes I didn't come home until the next day. I knew I wasn't going to stay married. Then I met Maggie.

MAGGIE: I had three kids and was separated from my husband, a Cleveland fireman. I was trying to make ends meet by selling Avon makeup, and I was depressed because of my marriage problems. I never went to bars, but my girlfriend, who was a distant cousin to Phil, insisted I get out with her on the weekends. We were at the Redwood one evening and she introduced me to him. I talked to him for a while. I didn't know anything about him. He was good-looking with a strong jaw, thick dark hair, and a great build. And he just seemed like a nice guy.

Two days later my girlfriend told me that Phil wanted to call me. I said no, but she gave him my phone number anyway and he called me. Phil was a smooth operator. He said all the right things. Pretty soon we were sneaking around together. I was very comfortable with him, and he made me feel special.

PHIL: I had been seeing Maggie for about a month. Sandy had already had it with my lifestyle, but this put her over the top. She filed for divorce, and I moved in with my mother and father. But that didn't last long because my father was always getting on my case about staying out all night. Maggie's husband had just moved out, so I wound up moving in with her and saw my son on the weekends.

MAGGIE: I was just nuts about Phil. He was good to my kids, and they thought he was cool. Not long after Phil's divorce, I got divorced, too. Phil treated me like a princess. He took me to Florida, bought a boat, and took my kids and me for rides on Lake Erie. Eventually we got engaged, and he bought me a big diamond ring. I wondered where he got his money, but Phil never told me anything about his work.

We would go out to a nice restaurant or nightclub with Charlie Broeckel and his wife. Charlie would always be whispering in Phil's ear, which really annoyed me. Sometimes Charlie would pick him up, and they'd be gone the whole day, sometimes even overnight. Phil would just say he had something to take care of. I knew not to ask any questions.

Chapter Four

PHIL: While I was living with Maggie, construction work slowed down, but Al Walsh and I got good jobs at the federal building downtown. I was the union steward, and Al was the general foreman. Then the trouble started again at the union hall. Paul Lyons got in a shouting match with Walter Moore and shoved him. Tommy McDonald, the head business agent, wanted Paul Lyons taught a lesson.

Al Walsh and I knew that Paul was working on a blast furnace, then hanging out at a certain bar afterward, so we left work at the federal building and drove to the bar. We both had guns on us. Al was going to tell Paul we wanted to talk to him outside.

The joint was loaded with guys who'd just got off work, but we quickly spotted Paul Lyons and a few of his friends at the end of the bar. I was watching them and following Al up to Paul Lyons. Suddenly Al backed into me, then I heard a shot. I pulled my gun out of my waistband and was looking at everybody to make sure they didn't come toward us. Then Paul Lyons slumped to the floor. I thought Al had just shot him. All of the guys in the bar were motionless with looks of horror on their faces.

Then Al said to Paul, "You're a dead mother-fucker."

Al put the gun right up to Paul's chest. I thought, no, not now, not here. But Al pulled the trigger. For some godly reason, it didn't go off. I grabbed Al's arm to lead him out, but he pulled the trigger again. It still didn't go off.

I yanked Al away from Paul and said, "Let's get out of here."

I still had my gun out as we backed out the door. We walked to the parking lot and got in the car while I made sure that nobody was following us. A couple of guys came to the door of the bar but didn't come out.

We got into the car and headed back to the federal building. Al was looking at his gun, and I asked him why he tried to shoot Paul.

Al said, "He saw us and must have known what was coming. He reached toward his foot, so I thought he had a piece in an ankle holster. I hit him in the head with my gun so hard that it fired. But I think the firing pin bent, and I couldn't shoot again."

I told Al I was glad his gun didn't go off. We would have been in big trouble if we'd killed Paul in front of all those people. Al agreed with me.

"Well, at least it didn't happen, and we put one hell of a scare in him," he said. "I bet that's the loudest click that cock-sucker ever heard."

"Yeah, you're not kidding. He's probably wiping his ass."

We both knew there'd be some shit over this. Sure enough, the following week Paul's guys went by Walter Moore's house and shot through his windows. Then Al's car got bombed. We looked for Paul Lyons high and low for a week. Al and I were going to make sure he couldn't hurt anybody again. We had two baseball bats and were going to break him in pieces and figured this would do the job. But Paul went into hiding. We went to his house at all hours of the night, and his car was never there. We checked all of the bars where he hung out, and nobody had seen him. He didn't even go to work.

We quit looking and figured he would eventually come out of his hole. We just didn't know if it would be with a bomb or a gun. Then Tom McDonald called Al and me into the office. He gave us two thousand dollars each and told us to lay off Paul for now because there was a lot of heat from the law.

During pauses in the Iron Workers battles, I spent more time getting established as a burglar. I was developing a pool of associates to select from for certain scores depending on their expertise, but my main crew included Mario Durant, Herman Holly, and Charlie Broeckel.

I was very close with Herman, who was from the mountains of West Virginia. He spoke with a drawl, was tall and wiry, and had light brown hair that seemed to go in every direction except straight. Herman grew up poor, but when he started working with me, he was able to enjoy life. He bought a motorcycle and a boat, and took very good care of his wife and daughter.

Herman was very polite and kind, but he wasn't afraid of anything. He would call me Mr. Phil and was a great worker who I could trust to handle anything on a score. I would tell him to do this or that, and he would just pounce on it.

Eventually Charlie Broeckel became my best friend and partner. He was also my confidant. There weren't many things I wouldn't share with him. He was a few years older and would sometimes introduce me as his younger brother. Charlie could have been in movies, he was that good looking—tall and thin, with blue eyes and blond hair that he combed straight back. He also dressed sharp and drove a sky-blue Cadillac convertible.

Like many of the guys I ran with, Charlie loved to gamble. He would bet on anything and was always losing. One night we came off a score and cut up thirty thousand dollars. Then I went home and Charlie went down to Little Italy. The next morning he called me at three o'clock and woke me up to ask if he could borrow five thousand dollars because he'd lost all his money at barbut, the Greek dice game.

Charlie was reckless in other ways, too. When we would go into a big hardware store to buy tools we needed for a score, Charlie would steal something. I would tell him we didn't need to draw unnecessary attention to ourselves. But the next time we were in a store, he would take something again. He was a kleptomaniac.

He was also paranoid and high-strung. The guy couldn't sit still. He always had a cigarette in his hand and was always coughing. When his hair started turning gray, we called him the gray ghost because one minute he was with you and the next minute he was gone. He used to pop black beauties to keep himself up at night, then drink alcohol to calm himself down. And he always carried a gun on him and wouldn't hesitate to pull it out and use it. You would have never guessed he used to be an altar boy. He was a powder keg waiting to go off.

One time we were in a bar, and Charlie went to the bathroom. When he came out, some guy was talking to Charlie's girlfriend. Charlie said something, and the guy started acting like he wanted to fight. Before I knew it, there was a loud crack, and the guy fell to the ground yelling and moaning. Charlie had shot him in the leg. I hustled Charlie out a back door, threw his gun on the roof of another building, and drove him home.

Another time we were in a Youngstown bar. Charlie was drunk when some guy started arguing and getting him mad. I was watching him close and knew what was going to happen. Sure enough, Charlie pulled his gun out and aimed it right at the guy's chest. I pushed his arm up fast, just as he pulled the trigger, and the bullet went into the ceiling. The women customers were screaming, and Charlie was yelling at me as I hurried him out of the bar and took his gun. The next day he thanked me for keeping him from killing someone.

I never carried a gun in a burglary. I never felt the need to. But when we were on a score, I liked knowing that Charlie was covering my back while I worked on the alarm or safe. I trusted him with my life.

In the summer of 1965, I was called in front of the Labor Relations Board. I was the only one called. They wanted to know how I'd gotten my union card and if I'd served as an apprentice like everybody else. I had been told by Tommy McDonald that if the Labor Relations Board officials asked me these questions, I should tell them to see our union attorney. I did, and they were mad. They told me they would have me back in front of them and that it wouldn't stop there.

A week or two later, a bunch of us were subpoenaed by a grand jury. I guess the police had had enough of the battle and started an investigation.

There were about fifteen of us, including Al, Tommy McDonald, Walter Moore, Paul Lyons, and Richard Callahan. This was the first time we had come face to face with Paul Lyons since Al's car had been blown up. Paul came into the courthouse all smiles and smelling of booze, and put his hand out, which we didn't accept.

One by one, we went in front of the grand jury. Our attorney told us to take the Fifth Amendment no matter what they asked and gave us a copy of the words to say. When it was my turn, I went in and sat down. A clerk asked me to raise my right hand and began swearing me in, asking if I would tell the truth. I then proceeded to take the Fifth Amendment, reading from the paper the attorney had given us. The jury foreman told me I could say "I do" when the clerk swore me in. But again I read from the paper and took the Fifth. All of the jurors started laughing. The prosecutor, John T. Corrigan, got mad and said he was through with me for now. He said he might call me back.

I left the grand jury room, and Al was called next. He asked me for the slip of paper to read from. The other guys wanted to know what had happened inside, and I told our attorney that when the clerk asked me to swear on the Bible, I took the Fifth Amendment. The guys started laughing. The attorney said, "You aren't supposed to take the Fifth Amendment to that." I said, "Well, you told me to take the Fifth Amendment to everything they asked, and I did."

Ten minutes later, Al came out and I asked him how it went. He said it was good that I'd given him the paper with the Fifth Amendment on it. The prosecutor had asked him where he got the piece of paper from, and he told him from me. The grand jurors got a good laugh.

All of us who were subpoenaed did appear but were never called back. The investigation went nowhere because nobody would talk.

After the grand jury hearing was over, Paul Lyons came crawling to Tom McDonald because he was scared. Then Tom called Al and me into the office. He told us to lay off Paul because of the heat from the police. "Just lay back and see what happens," he said.

After that, Paul started coming around the union hall and even came into our neighborhood where we all hung around. After a while, the feud died down and union business was going smoothly. Then Paul started hanging around with some new people on the West Side. He thought he was a big man and started his same shit again. He'd come to the union hall drunk and get into arguments with the business agents.

Then one evening I got a call from the barmaid at the Redwood. She told me Paul Lyons had come down with a couple of guys, and they were starting trouble with some women customers and refusing to pay for their drinks. I was furious that he would invade my territory, but I wasn't going to take any chances with Paul like I had in the union hall. He must have had something on his mind to come to Collinwood all the way from the West Side. And so I grabbed a sawed-off shotgun that I kept in Maggie's closet, loaded it, and rushed down to the bar.

I went in through the rear door and saw that there were about fifteen people in the bar. Paul was sitting at a table with two other guys. I walked along the back of the bar to the end where the barmaid was and whispered for her to go to the other end. I had the shotgun down at my side. Paul Lyons turned around and saw me. He gave me a real big smile.

"You guys have had enough," I said loudly.

All of my customers stopped talking and were watching. Paul got up and walked toward me. When he got close, he saw the shotgun down at my side. He stopped in his tracks, and his phony smile disappeared for a second. Then he started joking with me in an Italian accent.

"Paisan, whatsa matter witha you?"

"There's nothing wrong with me, Paul," I said. "You guys can't come in here drunk, bother my customers, and tell the barmaid you aren't going to pay for your drinks."

"Aw, we're just kidding. We'll pay for our drinks. We're not bums."

"Forget it," I said. "Just get out of here. And don't come back."

Paul said, "There's no trouble. We're gonna leave, paisan."

He stood there looking at me for a few seconds. He glanced down at the shotgun, which I still had at my side. I was staring him right in the eye, waiting for him to make a move. If he tried anything, I would have killed him right in my bar. Nobody was making a sound. You could have heard a pin drop on the bar floor.

Then Paul turned to his two friends and said, "C'mon, let's go."

I just stood there at the end of the bar until they were out the door.

Two days later I heard sirens early in the morning but didn't think anything about it. It was Labor Day, and I was going to take Maggie and her kids on a picnic. I was outside, and this guy I knew came by and told me that the fire department was at the Redwood. He said they were inside the bar, too.

I jumped in my car and raced down to the Redwood, which was only a minute away. As I pulled up and parked my car, I saw a bunch of fire engines and police and detective cars. I walked up to one cop and told him I owned the bar. The cop said, "You better stand back like everyone else."

"Why do I have to stand back here? Isn't the fire put out?"

"Oh, it's more than a fire."

I couldn't imagine what he meant. Then I saw some guy in plain clothes come walking out the front door of the bar carrying something with both hands. He put it in the back seat of his car. Then a detective came walking up to me.

"I guess you have some enemies out there, Christopher," he said.

He knew my name.

I said, "Enemies? I don't have any enemies."

"Well, I'm sure no friend did this."

The detective took me in the bar and showed me what had happened. It smelled of smoke, and my beer cooler was destroyed. There was a small hole in the floor, and little bits of ceiling tile and dust were all over that side of the bar. The detective told me that somebody had planted dynamite under the cooler. Another bomb by the front wall didn't go off. I figured it had to be Paul Lyons.

Well, Maggie and I didn't go on any picnic. I had to clean up the mess in the bar. I was so mad the whole day I could have chewed nails.

A few weeks later, I was tending bar at the Redwood, and Al Walsh was sitting at the bar having a drink. Things were dead, so I said I'd close early and we'd go get breakfast. It was about one-thirty in the morning when Al went to get his car, which was parked on the street, and I went to get mine from the back lot. I had just opened my door to get in when I heard this car come pulling into the lot. I figured it was Al, but I glanced over my shoulder and saw it wasn't him. It was a dark-colored Ford, and someone was leaning out the back window. I saw a flash of light and heard a bang. I dove into the front seat of my car as my back window exploded. Then I heard another bang, and some more glass shattered on me. The car squealed out of the lot. A few seconds later, Al came flying in. He jumped out of his car and asked me if I was okay. Except for a few little cuts from the glass, I wasn't hurt.

The police must have been close because they came screeching in a minute later. One of the cops asked me what happened, and I told him I was going to my car when someone shot at me.

"You guys will just kill yourselves, then we won't have any problems."

He obviously knew about the war going on in the Iron Workers.

Then he stormed off without asking if I was okay. I had to laugh. I'd almost been killed, but he was mad.

Not long after, I heard that Paul Lyons's wife had been killed inside their home. Some people thought the idiot either had her murdered or had done it himself. A few months later, Paul himself turned up dead. Nobody was arrested. I felt bad for his kids, who were left all alone.

I decided to leave the Iron Workers, because it wasn't worth having all those battles for a job. Instead I started concentrating on the world of burglary. I continued learning a lot about alarms and safes, meeting people in the business and going on scores.

Chapter Five

From 1968 through 1972, Phil, along with Charlie Broeckel and the rest of his crew, was hitting drug stores, jewelry shops, post offices, and supermarkets in Ohio, Pennsylvania, New York, Florida, and California. Phil was quickly becoming known as a master burglar who could bypass any alarm and break into any safe.

The typical score went like this: Phil would get a tip about a target location that was in a good position as far as access and escape routes, and which was believed to house a large amount of cash or jewelry. Phil would build an alarm box, the kind he had perfected while practicing his burglary skills in the back room of his friend's private club. Essentially a switch used to "jump out" or electronically fool the security system, the alarm box would prevent a signal from being sent to the alarm company.

A getaway driver in an untraceable "Joe Blow" car would transport Phil, Charlie, and one or two lookouts to the score. The lookouts would stay outside, watching for police, security guards, employees, or potential witnesses. The men would communicate by walkie-talkie.

One of the lookouts would monitor a police scanner. If no burglary call was broadcast after Phil bypassed the alarm, then Phil and Charlie would go after the safe. Armed with a pistol, Charlie would cover Phil and assist with tools. Phil would break into the safe by either drilling it open or "burning" it with an acetylene torch. After successful burglaries, the crew would meet at the Redwood to celebrate.

The Cleveland Police Department had a burglary investigation unit with eight-by-ten photos of Phil on their office wall. The detectives worked with investigators from the Cuyahoga County Sheriff's Office conducting surveillance of and developing intelligence on northeast Ohio thieves. As the region's burglary rate swelled, local and state law enforcement officers focused attention on the burglars at the Redwood. Their photos were added to the mug shot field books carried by patrol officers and were also posted in turnpike tollbooths. The attendants had instructions to notify the Highway Patrol if they saw any of the burglars passing through.

Phil had mastered alarms and safes, but now he had a new challenge in his career. It was a challenge that would dog him relentlessly: the law.

PHIL: All those years, I'd been making a middle-class living. But there was no way I was going to work a nine-to-five job like a regular guy and wait forty years to retire. I wanted more out of life. I wanted a nice house and a new car, and I wanted to travel. But I knew it was going to take money. Money was king. I was totally determined to make it, and there wasn't any alarm, safe, or police department that was gonna stand in my way. Danger had become my middle name. But I wasn't reckless.

Some criminals preferred robberies. Stick a gun in someone's face and take their wallet, or hold up a liquor store. I never had anything to do with armed robberies. I preferred burglaries of businesses that were closed. There were no people involved, and all you had to contend with was an alarm system and a safe. And the owners would get reimbursed anyway by the insurance companies, which were thieves in their own right.

I never cared for house burglaries, either. I went on some, but only if I knew there was a safe in the house, an alarm, and nobody was home. If there was no safe and no alarm, then there was little chance of anything valuable being there, unless you had inside information.

As my connections grew, I got to know two Canadian robbers pretty well. Their names were Jimmy Minor and Tommy Terrin. Jimmy looked just like John F. Kennedy. Tommy was about five foot ten and a little on the heavy side. Both were clean-cut. Jimmy and Tommy were well-known in Canada, so they'd come into the United States periodically and do a couple of robberies to make some cash. They didn't need to wear masks because their photos weren't on file here.

I told Jimmy and Tommy that if they ever saw anything in Canada that would be a good burglary, then I would go up and take a look. In 1970, Jimmy called me and said he was looking at something big. He asked if I could come to London, Ontario, to take a look. He sounded excited, and he wasn't the excitable type. So I knew it must be something good.

The next morning I was on a twin-engine propeller plane headed for London. During the short flight, I was trying to imagine what sort of security there would be on the ground. I figured that once I landed I would just have to show my driver's license and go through immigration and that would be that.

The airplane landed, and we all got off. I stood in line and watched everybody show identification to uniformed inspectors who looked in some of the passengers' carry-on luggage and let them pass through. When it was my turn, I gave them my license. The inspector looked at it and asked if I had any luggage. I answered no and told him I'd just come for the day and would be going right back. Then he asked me what kind of business I had in London.

"Sir, what are all the questions for?" I asked. "Is there some sort of problem?"

"Would you mind stepping out of line and following me."

Now I knew something was wrong, but I played dumb. The inspector led me to an office and told me to sit down. A minute later another guy came in, about six feet tall and dressed in a dark suit. He had a French-Canadian accent and introduced himself as the head of airport security. He sat down at a desk across from me, and while he was looking at my driver's license, I was thinking about the question the uniformed guy had asked me about what kind of business I had in London. If this guy asked the same thing, I was just going to say I'd come over to get some souvenirs to send to some friends. I didn't have any luggage, so I couldn't say I was on vacation. And I certainly couldn't say I was coming to see Jimmy or Tommy.

The security director started asking me a bunch of questions. The spelling of my name, where I was from. Then, sure enough, he asked why I was in Canada. I told him I'd come to buy souvenirs and asked if there was a problem. He didn't answer. He had a wooden box in front of him, which had five inch by eight inch index cards in it. He looked through them, pulled one out, and read it. Then he looked up and glared at me.

"Are you sure that's all you came for, Mr. Christopher?"

"Of course, I'm sure. Why? Is something wrong?"

"Do you know anyone in London?"

"I don't know anybody. And I don't understand what all these questions are all about. I haven't done anything wrong."

"Are you sure you don't know anybody in London?" he asked again, while looking at the index card.

"Of course, I don't."

"Do you know Jimmy Minor or Tommy Terrin?"

I couldn't imagine what was on the index card or how he knew about Jimmy and Tommy.

"I don't know what this is all about, but like I said, I do not know anybody here."

His voice was getting higher and louder, and he asked me again if I knew Jimmy or Tommy. I wasn't going to get myself in any deeper.

"Listen," I said. "I answered your questions. You're not going to put words in my mouth."

He stared at me, and I looked right back at him. I thought he was going to say something, but he started writing something. Then he called someone on the telephone and told them to come over. A few minutes went by, and two London policemen came in the office. The security director told me he had to detain me until the matter was cleared up.

"This is ridiculous," I said. "There is nothing to clear up, because I didn't do anything. I'll just get back on the plane and go home."

"The only place you're going is to a Canadian jail."

The security director told the policemen to take me to their precinct. They handcuffed me and walked me out to the car. I was fuming by now. As we started to pull away, I saw Jimmy and Tommy standing on the sidewalk next to a pillar, like they were hiding. They saw me looking, and Jimmy gave me a sign that everything was okay, whatever that meant.

When we got to the police station, the officers brought me inside and down three iron steps to an old dingy area. There was this big pod that had six different cells in it with one cot each. I was the only prisoner and was locked in a small cell. I just walked around in circles, wondering how they knew who I was coming here to see. Either Jimmy and Tommy's phone had to be bugged, or they'd told someone and that person had informed the police.

A couple of hours passed, and two plainclothes officers—detectives I figured— introduced themselves. They brought me into a room with one desk and started questioning me. Two uniformed officers watched.

One of the detectives said, "You came here to see Jimmy Minor and Tommy Terrin, is that correct?"

I told him no.

"And you don't know anybody here?"

"No, I don't know anybody here."

"Then you tell me how one of the best lawyers in Ontario knew you were here in jail and called to find out what the charge was? We know you were here to meet with Tommy Terrin and Jimmy Minor. We will let you go if you tell us what business you had with them."

I didn't answer. Then they handed me this paper and told me they wanted me to sign it. It was a deportation order and said I promised never to come back to Canada or I'd be arrested. When I said I wasn't going to sign it, one of them snatched it from me.

"Put the irons on him," he told the uniformed cop.

"The irons?" the officer asked.

"Yes. The irons."

I was trying to figure out what their next move was, where they were going to take me, and what the irons were. This cop came out with some handcuffs, ankle-cuffs, and a chain. He put the chain around my waist and hooked the handcuffs to the chain. He went to put the cuffs on, and I stiffened up to make it more difficult. He got the cuffs on me, then put the ankle cuffs on and connected them to the other end of the chain.

The detectives left the room for a few minutes, then came back in and said, "Let's go." I got up and could hardly walk, but they were purposely rushing me. I shuffled along out the door and to a police car. They opened the back door and I got in. After we started moving, I asked them where we were going.

One of them said, "You will see when we get there."

We passed a couple of stores I had noticed when they brought me from the airport to the police station. I figured we were heading toward the airport. Sure enough, we got to the airport, and they pulled through a gate and up to a building near the runway and boarding area. They stopped the car and told me to get out. It was hard getting out of the car, and of course, they didn't help me. They just stood there and watched.

The detectives were looking at a propeller plane, like the one I'd flown in on. It was about one hundred yards away, and people were climbing the steps and getting in. When everyone was on board, one of the detectives walked over and stopped by the bottom of the steps. He talked to someone who looked like he might have been the pilot or co-pilot, then he pointed toward me. The detective by the plane waved to the one by me. He grabbed my arm and said, "Let's go." I had to shuffle all the way to the plane, which had both propellers going now. When I got there, they took off my handcuffs, ankle-cuffs, and chain.

They asked the pilot where he wanted me to sit, and he told them in the back of the plane.

One of the detectives said to me, "Sit in the back and don't cause any trouble."

The other detective said, "And don't come back."

I got on the plane and took a seat in the back. I was glad to be getting out of there. It didn't take long to get back to Cleveland. After I got off the plane, I was walking towards the door of Cleveland Hopkins Airport. Right inside the doorway, I saw two Cleveland police detectives I knew.

One of them said, "Did you have a nice time in London jail, Christopher?"

Then they both started laughing. I just kept walking past them. I thought to myself that the laugh would be on them in the end.

Chapter Six

The day after being kicked out of Canada, I picked up some cases of liquor and brought them to the Redwood. I'd been spending more time at the Redwood because I no longer had three partners. First, Al Walsh got married and moved to California. Then I kept finding money missing from the bar. I thought it was the employees and started watching, but I found out that one of my own partners was stealing from the bar. I couldn't believe he would steal from me, and so I threw him out, leaving only one other partner to help me run the bar.

While I was at the Redwood, Jimmy Minor called, and I told him about the whole ordeal. He said he had called one of the best lawyers in Ontario to see what they had me for, but the London police would only say that I wasn't charged with anything. Jimmy couldn't believe what had happened. I suggested that someone he knew was feeding the police information. He thought my phone might be tapped.

Jimmy asked me if I was going to come back. I told him I wanted to, and he suggested I go to Detroit, then take a bus through the Windsor Tunnel. He said that immigration inspectors weren't too sharp on people who came in by bus. I told him I'd be up the next day.

The next morning I flew from Cleveland's Burke Lakefront Airport to Detroit, then took a bus through the Windsor Tunnel into Canada. I got through the gate without any problem, then walked a little down the street and saw Jimmy and Tommy waiting for me. As soon as we shook hands, we started laughing about the ordeal in London.

Then we got in their car and started driving. I'd always heard that Canada was beautiful, and it sure was. We finally made it to the score—a bank that was supposed to hold $2 million in cash. Tommy said it was one of the richest banks in Canada because of the wealthy people who lived in the area. I said that sounded good to me.

We rode around, and it looked to me like the bank was situated nicely. "Let's go inside," I said. Tommy and I went in, and he cashed some bills for change while I looked around. I couldn't see any motion detectors, infrared eyes, ultrasonic or sound devices. Then we walked outside and around back and saw that the telephone wires were down low and easy to get at. There was hardly any traffic near the back of the bank, and there were a lot of woods and no houses. As Tommy and I walked back to the car, I told him it looked like a beautiful score. I was happy because I thought we could get really rich and lay back for a while.

We went back to Jimmy's place and started planning. We talked about how we would watch the bank, what tools we'd need, and where to get dynamite. Jimmy and Tommy told me they could get everything I needed. I would bring my alarm equipment with me when I came back.

That night we went back to the bank. Jimmy dropped Tommy and me off, and we disappeared into the woods. We wanted to know how much attention the police gave the bank. We watched from the woods, and the police only came through once. We did this two more nights.

Now that we saw how the police watched the bank, we talked about how many people would be involved. They had one of their guys from Canada coming in on the score. I told them I would bring two of my guys—Mario Durant and of course, Charlie Broeckel.

When I got home, I called Mario and Charlie and had them meet me at the Redwood. I told them about the bank in London, and they wanted to know when we were going. Then we had drinks and celebrated.

While I was at the bar, Jimmy called from Canada. He told me to go to another phone, a pay phone across the street. I went there and it rang right away.

"You all right?" Jimmy asked.

"I'm fine. Why, is there a problem?"

"Well, after we dropped you off in Windsor, we were driving back to Toronto and guess who stopped us? The Mounties. And they were looking for you. It's a good thing you got out of here when you did."

"How did they know I was there?"

"I don't know."

"Somebody around you guys must be telling someone something, because nobody from here knew I was there."

Jimmy said he would check it out and get back to me in a few days. A week later I still hadn't heard from him. I tried to call, but neither one of them answered. A few weeks after that, I found out that Jimmy and Tommy had been arrested for a robbery. They'd had a shoot-out with the police. Someone in their crew was killed, but Jimmy and Tommy were okay. I always figured they went to prison for a long time in Canada because I never heard from them again.

Chapter Seven

Not long after my experience in Canada, I was at the Italian-American Club on St. Clair Avenue in Collinwood when a friend of mine invited me on a score. The next morning we were at this rags-and-paper salvage company on Woodland Avenue. I was standing inside the box truck where we were about to unload the merchandise. The tractor trailer we were breaking into was backed up almost to the cargo door of the box truck. We broke the seal on the handle of the trailer and pulled the doors open.

Suddenly six guys with guns jumped out of the trailer, yelling, "FBI. You're under arrest!"

I stood still for about ten seconds. We were caught that much by surprise. Several more agents came out of nowhere and started handcuffing us. I glanced inside the trailer, and it was filled with boxes of Pepto Bismol. Then one of the guys I was with took off running, and an FBI agent with a shotgun yelled for him to stop. When the guy kept going, the agent fired once, and the guy went down. That was back when the police could shoot at any fleeing felon. As it turned out, the guy was only hit by one pellet of shot and was okay.

While we were lined up and handcuffed, I started laughing to myself. FBI agents jumping out of a Pepto Bismol truck struck me as funny.

I said to one of the guys next to me, "They could use this scene in a Pepto Bismol television commercial."

"What are you talking about?" he said.

"This whole thing is enough to give you an upset stomach."

I was put on probation for three years, but continued as a burglar. The thrill of beating alarms, safes, and the police was addicting. And to me, the reward of a big, fast buck was worth the risk of prison.

By the time Phil was twenty-nine, he was coordinating a network of professional burglars, petty thieves, mobsters, and tipsters. At various times, his team included alarm company employees and a police radio dispatcher. Phil was always willing to share profits with someone who could provide a special service—usually privileged inside information or protection.

PHIL: I made a connection with this guy named Frank, who worked for the ADT Alarm Company. I called him, and he agreed to meet me at a Manners Big Boy Restaurant after he got off work. That evening I sat down at the restaurant counter and had some coffee. Ten minutes later a guy with an ADT shirt on walked in. He sat down and ordered a cup of coffee.

"How are you doing, Frank?"

"I'm doing okay, but I'd be better if I could make some extra money," he said.

I thought, this is good because it looks like he's hungry for money and I can get him to do some things for me.

"Let's go and sit at a booth so we can talk," I suggested.

The waitress asked if we wanted something to eat. I ordered some French-fried mushrooms. Frank wasn't hungry.

"Phil, what can I do for you so I can make some extra money?"

"Why don't you start by explaining to me exactly what goes on at the alarm office and how everything works."

"When an alarm goes off, a flag drops on the board, it buzzes, and I look at the number on the board. I go to the file cards to see what the name of the business is, then I call the police and radio our ADT security officer to respond."

Once Frank started revealing how things operated, I knew I could get him to work with us. He told me he had all the files for the alarms on the East Side. The files told what kind and how many alarms were at a specific location. I asked Frank specifically what he could do to help us if an alarm went off.

"The only thing I can do is to take my time calling the police. I can't hide the fact that it went off because other people in the office will have heard it."

Once I started working with Frank, it was a reassuring to know that the police would be delayed if we set off an alarm accidentally.

Not long after Frank went to work for us, I made it a point to get friendly with a policeman, a patrol sergeant, who socialized off-duty in the Redwood. Later I had a third party approach him about making extra money as a lookout for some thefts. The sergeant agreed and eventually brought his supervisor, a lieutenant, on board. Talk about an insurance policy. I couldn't be happier.

Those cops helped make us a lot of money. During 1971 and 1972, they acted as lookouts for about ten burglaries. At a Superior Saving and Loan, we got one hundred thousand dollars in cash and American Express money orders. On more than one occasion, we set off the alarm accidentally, and one of them was outside backing off other officers who were responding to the area, telling them that they would handle it themselves. They would just call the other officers on their radio and tell them that they had heard the alarm and would take care of it or that they had already checked it out.

I had good insiders in Cleveland. But in L.A., another city I was active in, it was another story.

Chapter Eight

Phil pulled off quite a few burglaries in California. Aside from the money he made, he fell more in love with the mountains and coast every time he went there. He also enjoyed the familiarity of working mostly with Al Walsh and a crew of several other Cleveland-area burglars who had relocated to Los Angeles in the 1960s. They were Frank Velotta, Ray Ferritto, Julius Petro, and Bob Walsh, an ex-cop, who was no relation to Al Walsh.

Detective Ed Barr, a safe-burglary investigator with the Los Angeles Police Department, was also familiar with the relocated burglars.

DETECTIVE ED BARR: My contact with these guys began around 1968, when we received information from our intelligence division that a couple of safe-burglars had arrived from Cleveland. My partner and I always made a point of personally meeting out-of-town burglars at their new local address. It had a shock effect on most and let them know that we knew who they were. We would warn them that we would be knocking on their door if their trademark started showing up in Los Angeles. Frank Velotta and I got along well. He talked freely but never said anything incriminating. Ray Ferritto was polite but a cold fish. We arrested Frank and Ray about four times for safe-burn jobs at supermarkets and jewelry shops.

Al Walsh was arrested on a grocery store burglary. We arrested Bob Walsh on the supermarket jobs, also. He was kind of a wise ass. When we searched his house, we found his service revolver, which he had reported stolen. Julius Petro's apartment seemed to be the main meeting spot. Many times we started our surveillance from his address. Later, Petro's associates found out he was an informant for our intelligence division.

PHIL: In 1971, Al Walsh invited me out to California to go on a score with Frank "Skinny" Velotta. He said it would be well worth the trip. I got everything straight with the bar—who would open, who would close, and who would get done whatever needed to be done while I was gone. Then I left for California.

When Al picked me up at the Los Angeles airport, the weather was out of this world. As we drove to his house in the San Fernando Valley, Al filled me in on what was going on. He told me about a couple of scores they were in the middle of and had to drop in a hurry. I asked what the problem was.

He said, "You know how warm it is out here. Like during the summer in Cleveland when there's lots of people outside."

"Yeah."

"There are people everywhere the whole year out here. We got spotted a couple of times. The last time we had to ditch our equipment, and Frank lost his alarm box. That's why he had me call you. There's this other score, and it would take him too long to get another box together. We want to move on it now before they move the store because all the buildings around it are being torn down. The score should be easy. It's a privately owned safe-deposit box company, and a lot of jewelry salesmen put their jewelry in there.

"I never heard of a private safe-deposit-box company."

"There's a lot of them in this part of the country. And God only knows how much we're liable to get out of there.'

"That sounds good to me."

We got to Al's house and dropped off my suitcases. I said hello to his wife, mother, and son; then Al and I went right back out and drove to Skinny Velotta's apartment near Universal Studios. When we got there, Al pointed out two undercover officers watching the building. He said it was probably detectives from LAPD; he'd been seeing them more often lately.

"It seems they've been busting Frank's balls a lot lately," Al said. "We don't know what the problem is."

"That's great. I really didn't need to come walking into fire. I'm on probation and shouldn't have even left Ohio."

"Don't worry, Phil. We have some good connections here. You'll meet one of them now."

We went into the apartment building through a back door. Frank's apartment was all laid out with a glass bar with neon lighting and crystal glasses, glass tables, and colorful furniture. Frank and I shook hands. He was a tall, thin guy with brown eyes and thinning dark hair on top.

I smelled tomato sauce cooking, and I saw some guy with glasses stirring the pot. Frank introduced him as Jimmy. He was about fifteen years older, with dark brown hair, a medium build with a bit of a belly, and a big nose. Jimmy was very pleasant, asking me if I knew Jack Licavoli and some other mob guys from Cleveland. I told him I knew Jack and some of the other guys.

Bob Walsh and Ray Ferritto were there, too. I knew Bob from when he used to be a Cleveland cop. He was fired after he shot and killed some guy, but now he was a burglar and a hell of a con man. Ray was a burglar from Erie, Pennsylvania. He had a lot of connections with guys in the Mafia and was good friends with Ronnie Carrabbia, who was also a friend of mine.

We all sat down, except for Jimmy, who continued playing around in the kitchen and stirring the sauce. We talked about the score that I'd brought the alarm box for. Frank said it only had one alarm, and that he'd already found the wires in the basement of an adjoining building. Frank had made a key for the building, using an impression. I'd heard of this but had never seen it done.

I thought, this is really starting to sound easy. I asked when I could see it, and Al said we could take a ride right then if I wanted. Since everyone else had already seen the score, I went alone with Al.

While we were driving, Al said, "You see that guy Jimmy? That's Jimmy "The Weasel" Fratianno."

The name didn't mean anything to me.

"He's an up-and-coming boss in the mob and knows people all over the country. If we get into trouble, we can use him to get us out."

"That sounds good to me."

We got to the score, which was on the corner of a wide main road and a residential side street. The buildings around it were being torn down, and this one was supposed to go, too. It was an old, one-story building connected to a small office building in the back and stuck out like a sore thumb. And there was nowhere to run or hide. If anything went wrong, it could be a deathtrap, but because of all the money we could make, we decided it was worth the risk.

We drove around, and Al pointed out the side door of the office building where the alarm wires were. He parked the car down the street, and we got out and walked back past the front of the store. There was a sign on the front door that said the place was protected by ADT Alarm Company. We looked in and could see the vault, which was old and would be no problem to open. Then we walked to the side of the office building, and I didn't see any people around.

I said to Al, "Let's go down to the basement to see where the telephone box is."

We opened the door and walked down into the basement. There wasn't a soul around. When we found the telephone box, I took out my handkerchief so I could open it without leaving fingerprints. There were little paper tags hanging from the different wires and terminals. Most had phone numbers and business names. I pointed to one that said ADT.

"Nice of them to label the alarm wires for us," I said.

Al smiled and nodded. I closed the box and we left the building.

I couldn't believe there wasn't any activity in there. The offices must have been empty because the building was coming down. I could see why Frank and Al wanted to move fast before the place moved and maybe had a tougher security alarm and a better vault.

That evening we all met at a restaurant. There was a new guy there, about ten years older, with dark hair combed back and olive skin. His name was Julius Petro. I'd heard of him because he was from Collinwood, but this was the first time we met. I'd heard he was a crazy son-of-a-gun who did a lot of time in prison for armed robbery and was suspected of several underworld murders in Cleveland.

We all started discussing the score. I could tell by the conversation that Jimmy Fratianno wasn't going. I figured we were just going to throw him a percentage to help in case someone got caught. I didn't care because it was like having an insurance policy. Frank said he and Al would go in the building and jump out the alarm, then back off to make sure there were no problems. Ray Ferritto, Bob Walsh, and I were supposed to use the key and go right through the front door. Julius Petro would drop us off and pick us up when we called him on the walkie-talkie. We planned to move on the score on Saturday. This way, if we had any problems, we would have Sunday to continue working.

Saturday came, and Al and I met at Frank's place. We made sure all the equipment and tools were wiped down and free of fingerprints. Then, Frank asked me to show him how my alarm box worked. I said it was simple and asked him if he was sure he didn't want me to jump out the alarm. Frank said he would do it. I wasn't going to argue, because it was their score. I showed Frank my box, and he understood it easily enough.

It was starting to get dark. Julius left with Al and Frank first. Then I took off with Ray and Bob. We got to a shopping center a couple of blocks away from the score, parked the car, and waited for word that Al and Frank had jumped out the alarm. We had a walkie-talkie in our car, and Julius had one, too. Frank and Al had a walkie-talkie and a police scanner.

About a half hour later, Julius came pulling up with Frank and Al. They had jumped out the alarm okay. If Frank had done something wrong, the alarm company would have called the police by now. We got into the car with Julius, and Frank and Al got into our car. We pulled up to the front door of the safe-deposit box company, and I got out with the key and a bag of tools. I was hoping I wouldn't have a problem with the key.

Bob and Ray made sure I got the door open okay before they got out with the rest of the tools. The key worked fine. I unlocked the door and walked in like I owned the place. But as soon as I started heading for the vault, I heard Julius blowing the horn. I turned around and saw him waving his left arm out the window and yelling for me to do something. Bob was yelling something too, but I couldn't understand what they were saying. I started walking toward the front door, and they pulled away. I dropped my tool bag and went to the front door to see what the hell was going on. They were just turning down a side street. The only thing I could think of was that the law was coming and that's why they were yelling.

I opened the door and looked up and down the street, but I didn't see any police cars. I ran across the main road at an angle to the street where they'd turned down, so I could see where they went. I looked around, and now Julius was behind the safe-deposit box building. It was too late for me to go back because I heard sirens coming from all over. Julius pulled away from the safe-deposit box building and took off. I was on my own now, and the sirens were almost on top of me.

I headed into some back yards and started making distance between the law and me. I was running from yard to yard, and it seemed that everyone had a high fence or cement block wall I had to scramble over. These fences in California were a lot higher than the ones I was used to in Cleveland.

After running about a mile, I came out onto an avenue with a median. I stopped to catch my breath. Great, I thought. I have no idea where I'm at and don't have a walkie-talkie. Then I remembered I knew Al's phone number. I walked out to a main street and saw a little bar. There was a pay phone inside. I called Al's house, and his wife answered. I told her what street I was on and what bar I was at.

I told her to tell Al that my car broke down and that I would call her back in a half hour to see if he called. I knew all I could do was wait. I sat down at the bar and ordered a scotch on the rocks to relax. The bar was pretty sharp inside, but there weren't many customers. I noticed the ones that were there kept looking at me. I must have looked a little out of place. Twenty minutes later I called Al's house again, and his wife told me he was on his way to pick me up.

I finished my drink and decided to wait outside because I was uneasy with everyone looking at me. I saw Al's car coming down the street and breathed a sigh of relief. But then Al pulled up fast on the other side of the road and stopped suddenly. He was with Frank. They looked nervous and Al started yelling to me.

"Run down the street. Go through the back yards and we'll pick you up."

They couldn't make a U-turn because of the median. They took off and I thought to myself, wait, we already did this. I looked around and didn't see the law, but I did notice someone peeking out the window of the bar at me. I could see Al was driving away from me, so I figured I'd better get out of here quick. I headed into some back yards and started hopping fences again. I just couldn't figure out what was going on. Then I heard a helicopter approaching. It was an LAPD chopper and had a big floodlight shining down around the bar. Now I knew why Al had told me to run. I ran faster. The helicopter was flying low and in circles, with the search light shining all around.

It got right above me, so I ducked into an open garage. I peeked out and saw it was headed away from me, so I moved from the yards to the street. Then I saw a car coming. I couldn't tell if it was the law, so I hid behind a tree. When it got close, I saw it was Al and Frank. I whistled, and Al stopped. I ran fast, hopped in the car, and he took off.

"What the fuck is going on?" I said.

"We got a call on the scanner. The bar owner thought you looked suspicious and might rob the joint, so he called the cops."

Frank said, "They probably thought it was connected to the safe-deposit box company."

"What happened to the score?" I asked. "Did we get spotted?"

"There was call on the scanner of a burglary at that address," Frank said. "But it was probably a half hour after I jumped it out."

"Did you make sure the wires wouldn't come apart when you put the box on?" I asked.

"That's what I was thinking, but I know I made sure they were tight."

"Well, I guess that score is blown," I said. "What else do you guys have that we can make some money on? I didn't come all the way to California to go home without some money."

Al said he didn't have any scores picked out. But Frank told us he had something we could make a few thousand apiece on. He said it was only between the three of us and Jimmy the Weasel. Al and I said it sounded good. Frank said he'd talk to Jimmy, then get back to us.

The next morning, Al and I met Jimmy the Weasel at a coffee shop. Frank asked me if I wanted to place a package on some guy's business. I figured it would be an easy way to make some money.

"Yeah," I said. "I'll put a package on his place."

"I've got dynamite," Frank said.

"What is it?' Al asked.

"A dry cleaners," Frank said.

Jimmy told us the name of the dry cleaners and the street it was on. He said it was near the Los Angeles International Airport in a rich area. After we finished our coffee, Al and I left to check it out. There were a lot of people around, so we figured we couldn't just leave the package in the front door or someone walking by might get hurt. We went around back and decided to try the roof. It was too high, so we found a hardware store and bought a six-foot step ladder. We went back, and I went up the ladder onto the roof.

People were watching us, and we pretended like we were roofers talking about a leak. I found a good spot to lay the dynamite and went back down. Then we put the ladder in Al's car and discussed how we were going to do it. I told Al there was a bunch of open stacks going down in the guy's store. We could put the dynamite down one of the pipes. Al thought it was a good idea. And since we didn't want to be driving around with dynamite in the car, we decided to leave it on the roof during the day. Then we could just come back at night, light the fuse, and lower it down the pipe.

The next day Frank dropped off four sticks of dynamite, a blasting cap, and about five feet of fuse. Al and I got a few other things we needed and left for the dry cleaners. We were on the freeway, with Al behind the wheel and me in the passenger seat putting the bomb together. I had the dynamite on the floor and the other stuff between my legs. I attached the fuse in the cap and was taping the dynamite, when all of a sudden the car started vibrating and I heard, boom…boom…boom…boom.

My heart started pounding because I had been in deep concentration. I looked up fast and saw we were driving on the berm. Al swung the car back into the regular lane. I was pissed.

"What the hell happened, Al?"

"Sorry. I was watching you work and not looking at the road."

"You almost gave me a heart attack."

I tried to relax, and after a couple of minutes I finished putting together the dynamite. I told Al we needed a bag or something to put it in and some heavy-duty string to place it down the pipe because we couldn't lower it by the fuse.

We got to the dry cleaners, parked the car, and walked to a nearby drugstore, where we bought a duffel bag and some twine. Then we sat in the car while I attached the twine to the dynamite and put it in the bag. We were just ready to get out when a cop car pulled in the lot. But he just pulled through and back out to the street. We waited a few minutes to make sure he didn't come back.

We got the ladder out of Al's back seat and leaned it against the building, and I went up on the roof. Jet engines from planes taking off and landing at LAX were thundering overhead. I put the bag of dynamite behind an air conditioning unit and climbed back down. We laid the ladder against the side of the building in an alley so we wouldn't have to carry it in the car. We figured nobody would touch it.

We went back to Al's house, where I read the newspaper and Al watched television. When it was almost dark, Al and I went back to the dry cleaners. The area was pretty deserted. Al dropped me off and pulled away. I got the ladder and quickly climbed to the roof.

I got out the dynamite and lowered it down the pipe about ten feet. I held the fuse in my mouth while I tied the twine around the pipe. I lit the fuse and as soon as it caught, I let it go down the pipe. Then I called "ten-four" on the walkie-talkie. Al knew that meant to pick me up. He answered "ten-four," and I climbed down the ladder. I was already about fifty yards away when Al pulled up.

"You're fast," he said.

"I don't fuck around."

We drove about a half mile down the road, pulled over, and stopped. We had the windows open and were waiting for the dynamite to go off. After we heard the blast, we went to a pay phone and called Frank.

"Everything went good at the game," Al told him.

Frank said for us to meet him and Jimmy at this Italian restaurant in an hour. We got there, and Frank was at a table. It was a pretty high-class restaurant. Frank said Jimmy would be there in a little while. Out of curiosity, I asked Frank why they wanted this dry cleaners packaged. He said the owner was a big bookmaker, and Jimmy was trying to shake him down. Frank told me not to say anything, which of course,I wouldn't. Usually I couldn't care less about something like this, but I was curious.

Jimmy the Weasel came in, sat down, and gave Al and me envelopes with twenty-five hundred dollars each. Then we all ordered dinner. While we were eating, Bob, Ray, and Julius came in. They were looking for us and thought they got cut out of something. Frank assured them they weren't getting cut out of anything.

Bob Walsh got up to make a phone call, and when he came back, he told us that Mae West was sitting in a booth on the other side of the room. I wanted to see for myself, so I got up and walked past her. It didn't look like her. She was old and was sitting with a young, good-looking guy. I went back to the table and told the guys it didn't look like her, and we laughed about it. When our waiter came by, I asked him if it was Mae West sitting there, and he said yes.

After dinner Al and I went to the Four Roses, a topless bar in the Hollywood area. Al knew the owner, a guy named Phil from Detroit. He also owned another joint, the Palamino Club, where Ike and Tina Turner were appearing that week. Al and I would drop in these clubs when I was in town.

At the Four Roses, we saw Redd Foxx doing his stand-up routine while the girls took a break. I told Al it would be nice if Phil could get the girls to take a picture with me when the place closed. I could bust balls at home and show Charlie and the guys because topless dancing was unheard of in Cleveland. Redd Foxx left the stage, and Al and I sat at the bar watching four of the girls dance. There was a pretty good crowd. After a while, Al got up and I saw him talk to Phil. Then he came back to the bar and told me it was all set.

I thought we would wait until closing time to do it, but about a half hour later, one of the girls came up to me, grabbed my arm, and said come with me. I looked at Al, and he said go ahead. I figured there was a room in the back where we'd take the picture. I was wrong. The girl led me up some steps, right on stage, and sat me down on a stool. The audience was laughing and applauding. All I could think of was how embarrassed I was in front of all those people. Then the other three girls crowded around with their hands all over me. The guys were yelling, "Can I come up there too?" and "Give her a squeeze for me." Al and Phil were laughing hard. Another girl came out with a camera. Phil yelled to me, "Smile, Phil," and the picture was taken. The people were clapping and whistling.

I know my face had to be red because there were so many people watching. The first girl led me back down off the stage. Guys were still clapping and yelling things like "You sure are lucky." I tried to play it cool, but then I stumbled and almost knocked the girl over. It couldn't get any worse than that. I got back to the bar, and Al was laughing. Then Phil came with the Polaroid picture. I looked at it and figured the embarrassment was worth it. Then Al and Phil started laughing all over again about me almost falling down the steps.

"You should have seen your face when you tripped," Al said. "You looked horrified."

I started laughing myself, thanked Phil, and ordered a drink.

Chapter Nine

It was 1971, and my wild life continued. I was getting many calls from burglars and mob guys across the country who had scores with alarms and safes
they couldn't beat. These were smaller jobs I could find any time, but I'd tell them
I would take a look. I surely wouldn't throw a simple score out the window
because money was money. I always kept myself busy and wouldn't let any grass
grow under me. If you didn't hustle, you weren't going to get ahead. Most of these
scores were a piece of cake, and the money was great for the time invested.
Every now and then, someone would call me in on a bigger score, and of course,
those were more of a challenge.

One day I got a call from Ronnie Carrabbia. He was in Cleveland and
wanted to talk to me, and I figured it might be for a score. Ronnie was from the
Youngstown, Ohio, area, where many of the mob-connected guys I worked
with were from. At one time the area was divided into two territories—one run
by the mob in Pittsburgh and one by the Cleveland crime family. Ronnie
Carrabbia and his brothers, Charlie and Orlie, belonged to the Cleveland mob.
Tony Delsanter was their boss, and they were all under John Scalish, who had
been the boss of the Cleveland mob since the forties. I worked with mob guys

from both crime families, but I was closest with Ronnie Carrabbia.

Like many of the guys I worked with, Ronnie Crab was about ten years older. He was about six feet tall with brown wavy hair and a fair complexion. He didn't see too much afternoon sun because he was usually going to bed when the sun was coming up. That's the time the crap games, card games, or barbut action would end. Like many of my friends, he loved to gamble. If it wasn't gambling that kept Ronnie up all night, it was his bar called Tropics on Market Street in Youngstown.

When I went to Tropics, it was usually to meet Ronnie about a potential score. But there was a lot more going on at Tropics. The first and second floors of the club were decorated with abstract paintings of people in various sex acts and featured music, dancing, gambling, and gorgeous call girls at the ready. The basement floor was Ronnie's office.

Ronnie had his hands into everything and was making money by the bushel. But he was generous to his friends, treated everybody with respect, and was very much the gentleman. As people piled into his club, he would greet them graciously. Whenever we were out to eat, Ronnie would pick up the tab. After you were with him the first time, you left feeling like you'd met a long-lost friend. He had a lot of the local police officers and politicians in his pocket and knew important people in New York, Chicago, New Orleans, Kansas City, Los Angeles, San Francisco, and Las Vegas. Whenever they came into town, you could find them at Tropics with Ronnie.

After I got the call from Ronnie, I drove up to Jack Licavoli's joint in Little Italy to meet him. I walked into the little bar next to Roman Gardens Restaurant and found Ronnie, Jack, and Ray Ferritto sitting at a table. Butchie Cisternino, one of Jack's guys and a distant cousin of mine, was also there. They got up and we shook hands. Jack kissed me on the cheek and invited me to have some of his homemade wine.

I had first met Jack Licavoli in the sixties. Short, balding, and a little overweight, Jack spoke softly in an Italian accent and seemed to consider every word that came out of his mouth. I liked that about him.

On the table was a tray of bread, lunch meat, cheese, and olives. I had a little to eat and we made small talk. After about fifteen minutes, Ronnie motioned to me. We excused ourselves, walked outside, and stood on the sidewalk. A few guys I knew from that neighborhood were eyeballing us while we talked. They must have figured I was up there on business because I never went to Little Italy just to hang around. All you would get is heat from the law, and nobody up there was going to help you make money. They were wannabe mobsters, and all they did was hang on the corners and talk gangster talk. I did respect the older guys, but most of the younger ones were nothing but mouth. I was my own man, and I made my own money my own way, with nobody's help.

Ronnie started telling me about a score he had coming up in Albany, New York. There were some burglars I didn't know on the job, including Amil and James Dinsio, two brothers from Youngstown. Ronnie said it would be a very big haul but was very touchy.

"It involves some mob-connected people and politicians who've been raking money in for years."

"It doesn't matter to me, Ron," I said. "They bleed just the same."

"Listen, Phil, nobody can get caught because they'll be dead. But we're looking at as much as $10 million."

My eyes opened wide. I understood now what he meant about it being touchy. With that kind of money, I was sure it would be tough.

"When do we go?" I said.

"If you can come to Youngstown in a day or so, we'll all sit down and talk this out."

"Just let me know when and where. Hey, can Charlie come on the score with me if there's that much money to go around?"

"Well, there's six guys including myself, and you'll make seven. What the hell, bring him. One more won't make any difference."

I wanted to bring Herman Holly too, but he'd recently found out he had cancer.

Two days later, Charlie and I met Ronnie at a motel where he hung out, off the Ohio Turnpike outside of Youngstown. Ronnie was with Bob Walsh and Ray Ferritto. We went in the little restaurant and bar and sat down at a table near the window. Ronnie said we were waiting for the two Dinsio brothers and asked me if I knew them. I told him I'd never heard of them before he mentioned them the other day.

We sat there and had coffee, and after about a half hour we saw Amil and James Dinsio pull into the lot driving a new, red Cadillac Eldorado.

Ray Ferritto said, "They sure look like they're doing all right."

The Dinsios came inside, and Ronnie introduced Charlie and me to them. They were both about five feet eight inches tall, and muscular.

We moved to a motel room that Ronnie had rented, where he started telling us about the score. It was a house in Albany, New York, and the information came from the nephew of the owner—the person who had all the money. Ronnie said he was a big politician connected to the mob. There was a vault in the basement, and the house was supposed to have an ADT alarm system, which I was familiar with.

There was supposed to be only one guy in the house—an older man who would be nothing to worry about. They knew which bedroom he slept in, and of course, we weren't going to hurt him—Ronnie had promised the nephew that. The kid just wanted some of his uncle's money. So far, it sounded good.

Then Ronnie said the police in Albany kept a good watch on this guy's house. I didn't like that, but he said he had a plan. He said there was a strike going on with the telephone company in Albany. I couldn't figure out what effect that would have on the score. But Ronnie explained that the plan was to detonate some nitroglycerin, which he'd got from a friend in Canada, at a few of the unoccupied telephone company buildings. The police would think it was related to the strike. They'd be busy and wouldn't be making passes on the house for a while. It would give us enough time to get in and out before they knew what happened.

I said it sounded like a good plan and asked if there were police radios for that area. Ronnie said they had all the equipment, and we'd move on it in a couple weeks. Ronnie, Ray, Charlie, and I would be flying and meet the rest of the guys there. We covered everything, and Ronnie said he would call me to tell me when we were going to go. So I shook hands with everybody, and Charlie and I went back to Cleveland.

Chapter Ten

When we got to Albany for the score, Bob Walsh picked us up at the airport and drove us to a hotel where they had rented two adjoining rooms. Everybody was there, and we sat down and discussed exactly what we were going to do. There would be five of us to move on the house. Ronnie would drive. Amil, James, Charlie, and I would jump the alarms out and beat the vault. Jimmy, Bob, and Ray would set off the nitro in the telephone company buildings, which had already been picked out.

We decided to make a dry run on the house. Amil, Charlie, and I would check out the alarm system that evening. James would drop us off, and Ronnie would be roaming around in another car in case something went wrong. The rest of the guys would just wait, and the next day we'd move on the score.

That night all I had with me in the car was a little bag with my meter and a couple of tools to strip the wires back. Charlie and James had walkie-talkies. Ronnie had a walkie-talkie and a police scanner for the Albany police department. Amil was carrying two wooden pegs. I didn't know what they were for.

We made a couple of passes on the house, which was in a middle-class neighborhood and sat right on the corner of two streets—one being a dead end.

The street lights were pretty dim, which was good. There were no bright lights in the backyard, but there were some inside the front of the house. The house next to it was dark.

Amil told his brother to pull down the side street and drop us off at the dead end. Not too far from there was a freeway. We could head that way if anything went wrong. I always look to see which way I can run if need be. I got out of the car with Amil and Charlie, and we made our way through the backyards toward the house. Charlie checked with Ronnie and James on the walkie-talkies, and their voices came in clear.

The fences between the houses were easy to jump over, and a lot of them only had bushes. While we were cutting through the yards, some dogs started barking. We watched the houses where they were, and nobody looked out the windows. We got to the house next door and were standing in the dark. There was a big eight-foot chain-link fence between the houses. If we had to climb over the fence, somebody could see us easily and hear it rattle. We pulled up the bottom of the fence, and Amil put the two wooden pegs on the ground standing upright and about three feet apart. We let the fence down and it was now propped up by the pegs. If we needed to, we could slide under it quickly.

I went to the back porch with Amil and Charlie and pulled off the wood grating that enclosed the bottom. Then I crawled under and was just pulling out my little flashlight because it was pitch black. I heard Charlie say something, which I didn't understand. Amil tapped me on the leg and said come out. Charlie said he saw a cop car pull up slowly in front of the house and stop.

I put the grating back in place fast, and we went to the other side of the house. The cop was out of his car and walking casually toward the house. It appeared that he was just checking the house out. Amil went real fast under the fence on his belly. I went next and was looking toward the front of the house to see where the cop was going. I could see him because of the streetlight, but he couldn't see us because it was very dark in the backyard.

Amil and I were waiting for Charlie to come under the fence before we pulled the pegs, just in case the cop came all the way in the backyard. Charlie crawled under the fence with the walkie-talkie in one hand and his gun in the other. But he was coming under the fence on his back, not in his belly like Amil and I did. I grabbed the walkie-talkie out of his hand, and I was thinking he should have done like I did with my little bag. I had thrown it through the bottom of the fence, then crawled through. I looked up but couldn't see the cop now. He might be coming around the other side of the house.

Suddenly Charlie screamed. I looked down and saw that the fence had snapped down on him like a bear trap. It caught Charlie between his legs and he couldn't move. Amil and I pulled up the bottom of the fence fast. As we lifted, Charlie screamed again but was able to snake his way out. We looked up and could see the cop staring right at us from about fifty feet away. But he couldn't see us—he didn't have a flashlight. We could see him because of the streetlights.

He pulled his gun out and yelled, "What are you doing back here?"

Amil and I grabbed Charlie under each arm and dragged him into the backyard and out of sight of the cop.

Then the cop yelled, "Stop or I'll shoot!"

We dragged Charlie as far and fast as we could until we came to some bushes. We pulled him to his feet, but he couldn't move his legs. I put him over my shoulders and started moving as fast as I could. The cop never shot at us, probably because the fence was in the way. And he didn't chase after us since he was alone and it was dark.

When we came to another fence, which was about four feet high, Amil and I lifted Charlie over it. I was tired from carrying him. It's bad enough running from the cops, let alone carrying an extra two hundred pounds on your back. Amil carried Charlie on his back until we were by the freeway. Thank God the street wasn't too long until it reached the freeway. The weeds on the side of the freeway were high, so we flattened ourselves down on the ground and out of sight to catch our breath.

While resting a moment, we could see a spotlight coming from behind us by the dead end. The light brushed over us as we sat low in the weeds. Amil and

I were out of breath and sweating like pigs. Charlie was just lying there, holding his crotch.

He kept saying over and over, "My balls are ripped open. My balls are ripped open."

There was blood all over Charlie's hands. I could even smell it.

By now we were catching our breath. The light from the cop car was still searching the area around us, and Amil and I were saying we had to get to the other side of the freeway. We knew we had to carry Charlie across the freeway. We could hear James and Ronnie calling over the walkie-talkie. They knew we had problems and wanted to know where to pick us up. Amil and I didn't answer because we knew we had to move from where we were. We also figured that sooner or later a police car would make its way down the freeway and try to sandwich us in.

I asked Charlie if he could crawl. He said he was hurting too bad and couldn't even move. I knew I couldn't leave him there.

"We've got to get out of here," Amil said.

"I know, but he can't move."

The spotlight was still shining around. Then we saw a police car with its flashing lights on the other side of the freeway coming toward us. He stopped almost directly across from the other police car that was shining his light from the dead end. We were about fifty feet from both of the police cars. The cop on the freeway shined his spotlight around for about a minute, then took off with his flashing lights on. We knew he would be back down the freeway on our side soon.

"C'mon, Phil, let's get out here," Amil said.

"We'll be back for you," I told Charlie.

"Please don't leave me here, Phil."

"We aren't going to leave you. Just hang on. Amil and I will make it across the freeway and draw the cops away from you. We'll get picked up by one of the guys and come back to get you. The cops don't know how many of us there are. They'll leave you alone."

I could tell Charlie was in a lot of pain. I could also see the flashing light from the police car coming down the freeway toward us on our side. So Amil and I jumped up and started running across the freeway like two deer. Cars were zooming up and down. The spotlight from the cop at the dead end was now directly on us. Amil and I ran across freeway, hurdling the metal divider. I glanced to our left to see how close the cop car was, but now there were three police cars coming down the freeway. We made it to the other side, and there were more spotlights at our back. They more or less lit the way as we ran.

Then we heard gunshots. We were up the embankment and heading into a wooded area. We heard a few more shots but didn't stop to look around until we were deep into the woods and out of sight. We stopped for a minute to catch our breath, then took off again, stumbling as we ran fast to make a lot of distance between us and the police. I figured Charlie was all right because we drew the cops away from him. Now it was up to us to make it to where we could call on the walkie-talkie and have Ronnie or James pick us up.

Amil and I had been running parallel with the freeway for about twenty minutes. We hadn't seen any police cars for awhile, so we finally stopped to rest. We inched our way up to the freeway and stood behind some trees. Cars and trucks were flying by in both directions. We moved closer and crawled on our hands and knees in tall grass and weeds until we could see up and down the freeway. We didn't see any flashing lights. While we were squatting down, we spotted a police car. He was moving slower than the traffic but kept on going. We figured he was looking along the sides of the highway.

Amil and I thought we'd better give a call on the walkie-talkie. I had turned it off because I knew we couldn't talk while running.

I turned the radio on and said, "Testing one, two."

James answered, "We hear you."

Amil and I were trying to figure out how to tell them where we were.

I said over the radio, "We're on the runway, a few miles away from you. We'll be looking for you."

We figured they should know what we meant. And even if they went the opposite way while looking for us and we didn't spot them, they then would come the other way. The best thing we could do was sit tight and watch for their cars.

We kept watching the freeway as cars and trucks zoomed by. Another cop car went by, but he was moving at a normal speed. We figured they quit looking for us. I looked at Amil and noticed blood on his right shoulder.

"Amil, did you get shot?"

"He felt his shoulder and said, "No, I'm not shot. You've got blood all over you too."

I looked and saw blood on my shoulder and down my arm.

I said, "I bet we got this from carrying Charlie on our shoulders."

I hope he's all right, I thought to myself.

About twenty minutes later, we spotted Ronnie driving on the opposite side of the freeway.

I grabbed the walkie-talkie and said, "You just passed us. We're on the other side."

We could see Ronnie's brake lights come on for a second, then the car sped up.

James's voice came over the radio. He said, "We'll see you in a minute."

"I guess they're both in one car now," I said to Amil.

By now Amil and I were relaxed and laughing at all the falls we had in the woods as we ran. But we kept our eyes open to make sure there weren't any police cars around when Ronnie and James approached. A few minutes later, we saw Ronnie's car with its right blinker on coming toward us. As soon as they were alongside us, I said "Stop" over the walkie-talkie. Ronnie cut off to the right berm and skidded to a stop. Amil and I got up and ran like bullets while looking around for police cars. James opened the back door of the car on the passenger side, and Amil and I jumped in.

"Go, go, go," I said.

Ronnie took off before the door was closed and peeled out of there as Amil and I looked out the back window. We didn't know if the cops were behind us or not. Nothing was said for a few seconds as we kept looking out the back window. When we saw that we were all right, we relaxed for a minute as we went down the freeway on the opposite side from where we left Charlie.

"I leaned over the front seat and said, "Charlie got caught under the fence and it looks like he got his balls torn off. We have to try and pick him up before he bleeds to death."

Ronnie headed in that direction, and before I knew it, we were back where James and I had run across the freeway.

"That's where he is," Amil said. "Just about over there."

We pulled up near where we'd left Charlie, and I wondered if he'd still be there. If the cops had grabbed him, they might even be watching the area. We went down the freeway until there was a cutoff. We went up the cutoff and turned down the street, then went down the ramp on the other side of the freeway. We were all quiet as we looked to see if there were cops around. It was dark, and we couldn't see up and down the freeway very far. There could be a police car right behind us, and we wouldn't even know it.

Chapter Eleven

I told Ronnie we were getting close, and he slowed down a little. I could see Charlie's head from the lights of the car. He was sitting up in the weeds. "Over there," I said and pointed.

My heart was pounding again as I had my hand on the back door handle. Ronnie pulled onto the berm and turned the headlights off. I jumped out of the car and ran to Charlie, James following me. He was looking toward the dead end street for cops. I grabbed Charlie's arm, yanked him up and over my shoulder, and ran toward the car.

He was moaning as I just about threw him in the car. Ronnie hit the gas pedal, and the tires spun in the dirt until they hit the pavement. Then the car jerked forward.

Charlie was moaning, "Take me to a hospital. I'm bleeding to death."

I said, "Hang in there. We'll get you to a hospital."

Ronnie said he wanted to get some distance between us and the cops.

"Fuck the distance," Charlie said.

But I knew Ronnie was right.

'We'll be there soon,' I told Charlie.

He kept moaning and holding his crotch as if he'd been kicked. We drove about thirty miles, then pulled off the highway and into a gas station. Ronnie got out and asked the guy inside where the closest hospital was. He came back to the car and took off very fast. About ten minutes later, we pulled up in front of the emergency room. Amil and I looked like we had been in a war, so there was no way we could bring Charlie in. I told Ronnie that either he or James had to help him into the hospital. I asked Charlie if he could walk. He said he couldn't even move, let alone walk. Ronnie left the car running and walked into the emergency room. James slid over into the driver's seat.

Ronnie came walking back out with a wheelchair and a male nurse. It was pretty dark out where we were stopped. Ronnie came around the side door where Charlie was and opened the door. The lights inside the car didn't come on because we had taken the bulb out earlier. We did this on all of our scores.

The nurse was holding the wheelchair while trying to look in the back seat. Ronnie grabbed Charlie's arm to help him out of the car. I was trying to help from inside without letting the male nurse see me.

"Take it easy," Charlie groaned. "You're hurtin' my fuckin' balls."

The male nurse saw that Ronnie needed help. He and Ronnie got Charlie in the wheelchair. The nurse pushed Charlie toward the emergency room as he looked back at the rest of us. I know we looked suspicious, but there was nothing we could do. Ronnie came back to the driver's window and asked what we were going to do next. We told him we would be back in half an hour.

It was 4:00 a.m., and we drove around trying to find something to eat. Nothing was open, so we pulled into a gas station and got some pop and crackers. When we went back to the hospital, there was a police car by the emergency room door.

"We better get out of here," James said.

He made a quick U-turn, and we drove off. I leaned over the front seat.

"Do you think the cops have Charlie and Ronnie?" I said.

"We have to figure out how to find out," Amil said.

I suggested we call the motel to see if Ronnie left a message for us. James pulled off the road at the first pay phone we came to and called the room. Ronnie hadn't called. So we drove down the road to the hospital, but the police car was still there. We went back up the road again, turned around, and came back. Still the police car was there. We did this four or five more times, then finally the cop car was gone. We pulled in the back of the hospital and parked. James went in to see if Ronnie and Charlie were still there or if the police had picked them up.

James was in the hospital about ten minutes. He came out smiling, and I knew everything was all right. He was laughing and shaking his head when he got in.

"Ronnie is in there flirting with some nurse, and Charlie is getting his balls sewed up," he said.

We all laughed. I stretched out in the back seat and closed my eyes. I must have dozed off for a little while, then I heard Ronnie's voice outside the car. I sat up and saw him, Charlie, and a woman nurse standing by the emergency room door. We helped Charlie in the car. The nurse was shooting the bull with Ronnie and didn't pay any attention to Amil or me.

I asked Charlie how he was doing, and he said he felt like he just got castrated. He seemed to be in good humor and not in too much pain. Ronnie thanked the nurse, and we took off. I asked Charlie how he felt again. He looked drowsy.

"I've hardly got any pain. They gave me some good pain killers."

"What did they do?" I said.

"They put fourteen stitches in my balls cause they were open and hangin' out."

We were laughing hard now.

"Didn't you have to tell them how you did it?" I said.

"I told them I was drivin' on the freeway and ran out of gas and was walkin' to the first cut-off to get gas. And while I was walkin', I seen a gas station on the other side and jumped a fence. I told them there was barbed wire and it got between my legs, then I slipped and fell."

By now we were roaring. Ronnie said the doctor and nurse were laughing, too.

It was light outside when we got back to the motel. Ray Ferritto and Bob Walsh were up having coffee and donuts. They asked what happened and said they had been going crazy looking for us. They said there were police all over the place, and they were even in the motel parking lot checking license plates. We told them everything that happened, then I went to take a hot shower to wash the dirt and blood off.

We decided to leave later on that afternoon because we had to get some rest. After I took a shower, I flopped down on one of the twin beds and fell asleep as the rest of the guys were talking. The bed felt so good. It must have been 3:00 p.m. when I woke up. We finally checked out of the hotel and went to a Howard Johnson's to eat, then Charlie and I drove back to Cleveland.

I drove Charlie home, and he got out with his crutches. He hobbled up the sidewalk and into his apartment. Then his girlfriend saw him and went into a panic.

"Oh my God, Charlie, what happened?"

"He's okay," I told her. "You'll just have to lick his wounds."

The following week I went to Herman's house to see how he was doing. He was getting radiation treatments and had lost all of his hair. He'd also lost a lot of weight, which was bad because he was thin to begin with. He looked pretty skinny but seemed to be in good spirits. His wife was home, so we all sat down and bullshitted. I tried to give Herman some money for his family, but he refused it. So I gave it to his wife. I told her to take it or I wouldn't visit them again. She took the money and later went grocery shopping.

I told Herman about what happened to Charlie in Albany. We laughed so hard we almost cried.

"I can't wait till I feel better so I can make some scores."

"You'll be better soon," I said. "I sure miss your hillbilly ass. I need a good back-up."

I could tell that made him feel good, but I knew he didn't have long. I wish

I could have done more for him.

I left, and as I was walking to my car, his wife came back from shopping.

"If you need more money," I told her, "just give me a call and don't feel funny about it. One thing's for sure, money can't replace a friend like Herman."

She started crying, and of course, I felt bad.

"What am I going to do without him, Phil? I've tried to be strong for him, but I hurt so bad."

"I know. I guess all we can do is keep him happy and hope some miracle happens or they find some drug."

"The doctor gave him only another month. The cancer is all through his body."

"I thought the doctor gave him longer than that."

"He did, at first."

There wasn't anything else I could say. I told her to keep her chin up and that I'd be back soon.

Two months later Herman died. I really thought the world of him. It was like losing a brother.

Chapter Twelve

It was December 1971, and I was working on two scores. One was a savings and loan, and the other was a liquor store in Cleveland Heights. The liquor store should have been an easy one. There was no vault, only a safe. We figured there would be quite a bit of money in the safe because Christmas was right around the corner. And we were just going to snatch it and run.

I was with two other burglars for the liquor store score, one named Gordon and another we called Pepsi because that's all he drank. On the night of the score it was very cold outside, and there was a lot of snow on the ground. The three of us pulled up to the store in Pepsi's car and walked in through an alley that ran in the back. We got inside the store and, little by little, slid the heavy safe to the back door.

We were going to take it to Pepsi's garage to open it. All we had to do was pull the car up and get it in the back. Pepsi had already taken the rear seats out to make room. As I went to get his car, the snow was crunching under my shoes. The cold felt good because of all the sweating we did to move the safe. I walked like I lived in the area. It was about 10:00 p.m. Not too many cars were on the street, and I didn't see any law.

I got in Pepsi's 1960 Ford and made a pass by the front of the store. Then I turned down the side street and checked the alley. Everything looked good. As I turned into the alley, I knew this was going to have to be fast. I turned off the headlights and pulled the car to the back of the store. Just as I waved for them to start coming out, I saw headlights from a car coming into the alley very slowly.

I couldn't tell what kind of car it was, but I stopped and told them there was car coming. Pepsi said it was the law. Now I could see the dome lights on the car and two cops inside. Gordon and Pepsi turned and ran back inside the liquor store. I couldn't jump back in the car and drive forward because the cops were coming toward me. I knew it was time to start running.

I knew they could only go as far as where Pepsi's car was parked, but I heard them yelling to me to stop. By then I was moving like a deer. It was a good thing because they started shooting. The shots were loud, and I could hear the thuds and cracks of bullets hitting all around me. But I was a pretty good distance away by the time they started shooting. There were a lot of shots, then it stopped. I knew they must have emptied their guns at me. Finally I made it far enough and had some apartment buildings between me and the police.

When I came out on a main road, I didn't see the law. I had to get across the street because I knew they'd be looking for me on my side. I ran across fast, then hid in some bushes to look up and down the road for a few minutes. I was wondering if Gordon and Pepsi got caught. Three police cars drove slowly down the roads with their spotlights shining in the alleys of the apartment buildings on the other side of the street. I knew I'd made the right move.

I rested a little, then knew it was time to make some distance between me and the law. I started running through backyards and got pretty far from the score. I felt I was in the clear now but was a long way from home. I thought if I could get to a phone, I could call the Pointview and find someone to pick me up. But for now I was lost and cold.

I was walking up a residential street when I saw a car coming, but I couldn't tell what kind of a car it was. I thought I'd better walk up one of the driveways because if it was the law, I was sure they'd question me. The lights were on inside this one house. It must have been around midnight. As I was walking up the driveway, I looked toward the car and could see it was cops. They were slowing down. Either I would have to run or get to the front porch of the house and make it look like I belonged there. I thought I could tell the people my car broke down.

As I reached the front door, I figured the cops must have been watching me because they had plenty of time to pass me as I walked onto the porch. I pretended to open the door as I pressed the door bell. A woman came to the door. As she opened the door, I saw a man coming, too. They looked to be in their forties. I was dressed pretty nice that night and didn't look like I was out trying to steal a safe.

I told the woman my car broke down and I needed to make a phone call to get help. She looked toward the man who I figured to be her husband. The area I was in was pretty rich. I was surprised when they opened the door so quickly and didn't even put the porch light on. The man said I could come in to use the phone. I didn't look back behind me to see what the cop was doing. I just walked into the house, and the woman showed me where the phone was. Both of them were very polite.

I thanked them as I picked up the phone and dialed the Pointview where I reached a friend of mine named Eddie. I told him my car broke down, and he said he could pick me up in a half hour.

From where I was standing, I could see out their big picture window, and it looked like the police car was gone. I felt pretty safe now and was trying to be as calm as possible, but my heart was still pounding hard. I put the phone down and walked into the living room. I knew the couple was going to ask me questions. I was trying to think right away before they asked me.

The man asked where I was coming from, and I told him Collinwood. He said I was quite a way from home and asked where I was going. I told him I was out with some girl and had just dropped her off at her house on Cedar Hill and was on my way home. I could tell they started getting suspicious about my story and pressing for details.

"But why were you in this neighborhood? You were going away from Collinwood."

This guy was being a pain in the ass.

"Well," I said, "she lives on a side street, and I just turned off her street and thought I was heading back toward Cedar Hill. But these streets go in such crazy directions, and I really got turned around. And to make matters worse, my car broke down."

The wife was nice enough to speak up and help me out.

"You're right about that," she said. "These streets are weird in the directions they go."

That seemed to satisfy the husband's suspicions. The woman asked if I wanted some hot chocolate, and I said no, thank you. The television was on, and we were watching Johnny Carson. I was constantly looking out the front window for Eddie and for the law. As we sat there watching television, they made small talk. The man told me he and his wife were school teachers. We chatted about how cold it was and how much snow was on the ground. I kept smiling and trying to relax, but I was really on pins and needles. I couldn't wait to get out of that house.

I saw some headlights in the trees and was hoping it wasn't the law. As the car moved very slowly, I could see it wasn't a police car, but I didn't know what kind of car Eddie had. It stopped in front of the house, so I got up.

"I think my friend is here." The car turned into the driveway and stopped. "Thank you, I sure appreciated it."

"I hope you get your car started," the woman said.

On the way back to my car at the Pointview, I told Eddie about the score, getting shot at, and the people who let me use their phone. The whole time he was saying, "No shit, no shit, no shit." When we got to the Pointview, Gordon and Pepsi weren't there, so I went home. It was late and I was tired. I figured I would find out what happened to them tomorrow.

The next day I went back to the Pointview and found Gordon. He said when the cops were busy shooting at me, he went out the front door with Pepsi and ran the opposite way I did. He told me Pepsi called the police and reported his car stolen. The police called him later, told him the car had been used in a liquor store burglary, and gave it back to him.

I told Gordon how I got away and about the people helping me. He couldn't believe they took me into their house that time of the night.

"Then again," he said, "you do have that innocent look."

Chapter Thirteen

By the winter of 1971, I was getting tired of being a bar owner. I still had only one partner to help with managing the place. And he was limited as to how much time he could spend there because of his regular job. So I was running the whole show. Then I started having problems with the law.

My father happened to be at the bar with me when it started. A police captain came in and told me he heard I was going after hours. I asked him who told him that, but of course, he wouldn't tell me. I told him it was bull crap. Then he started hassling me.

"Let me see your liquor license, Christopher."

"It's up on the wall, if you want to see it," I told him.

"Go get it."

"Get it yourself if you want to see it."

My father said, "I'll get it."

I told my father, "Let him get it himself. I'm getting sick of his shenanigans."

"Shenanigans? I'll give you shenanigans," the captain yelled, then stormed out of the bar.

That night at about 2:20 a.m., two cops came and stood in the bar to make sure everyone was done drinking at 2:30 and the place was closed for business. This went on for a couple of weeks, then stopped. But then the fire inspector came in to check the building. He found violations in the restaurant, and we had to keep it closed until they were fixed. After that, the health inspector came down on us because we should have had two bathrooms upstairs for the bar and two downstairs for the restaurant. I felt like the law was just hassling me because I was a burglar. So I got mad and closed the restaurant down completely, then started thinking about selling the joint.

In February of 1972, my bartender called and told me that Amil was looking for me. When I got to the Redwood, Amil asked if there was somewhere to get a bite to eat, so I took him to a nearby coffee shop. We ordered sandwiches and started talking about different security systems and scores that had given us headaches. Amil said he'd been having problems with ADT. I told him it's a hard system to beat.

Then Amil asked me if I had ever done anything out west. I said I did and that it was a very touchy area because it's warm most of the time and you never know who might be walking in the dark and catch you doing something.

Amil told me he recently visited his nephew in California and spotted some nice scores. "There's two banks I really like. One's a United California Bank branch. The safe-deposit boxes should be loaded because it's in a rich area called Laguna Niguel."

"Sounds good to me."

"And get this, Phil. The other is the president's bank. You heard about the milk money?"

"No, what's that?"

"Nixon's got this big slush fund from the dairy farmers. It's illegal money he got for his campaign. And he keeps it in a safe-deposit box at this other bank in San Clemente, California. Supposed to be millions."

"If we hit that one, we'll have the whole Army after us."

We both laughed.

Amil told me his brother, James, and also his brother-in-law, Billy, were going to be on the score. I never heard of Billy. I told Amil that I had a crew I worked with, but when I moved with somebody else, I usually took Charlie Broeckel. Amil said he didn't mind Charlie coming, as long as he didn't get caught under any more fences.

Amil said his nephew, Harry, had a Joe Blow car with a false bottom in the trunk, and the tools could be transported to California in it. I asked him when he wanted to move on it, and he said he was looking into finding an apartment or condo for us near the score. As soon as it was rented, we could go.

When I got home, I called Charlie and told him to meet me at the Redwood. I told him about the score, and he was excited and wanted to celebrate. A few days later, Charlie and I took a ride to Youngstown. I stopped to visit some guys I knew but didn't tell them I was meeting Amil. If I did, they would know something was coming down and would be buzzing around trying to get in on the play.

Charlie and I met Amil and his brother at a truck stop off the Ohio Turnpike, and we discussed the score. We decided not to hit the president's bank because of all the attention it would bring. We'd move on the United California Bank in Laguna Niguel and start on a Friday, so we'd have the weekend to work. This was before banks were open on Saturdays. Amil's nephew in California had found a condo close to the bank. We decided to leave in four days. His nephew, Harry, was already on his way with the tools and the car. We also had phony driver's licenses being made, which Charlie was going to pick up.

I told Maggie that Charlie and I would be out of town for a couple of weeks. I said if anybody called to tell them I went bear hunting up in Canada. I didn't want anyone to know where we were. I knew in a few days guys would be looking for me and wondering if I'd left them out of a score.

The sun was shining on the day we left for California, but it was still typically cool for March in Ohio and there was a little snow on the ground. Just before we went to get our tickets, I asked Charlie for the phony driver's licenses. He left them at his house. I knew I should have taken care of it myself. When we went to get our tickets, we had to show identification. It was a new regulation because of all the hijackings going on. We all signed for the tickets using our first initials and last names. It crossed my mind that we were using our real names, but we didn't have enough time to go back for the fake licenses. And I figured the law couldn't prove you did something wrong just because you were in the area.

I made it through security without any problem. So did Charlie, Amil, James, and Amil's brother-in-law, Billy. This was the first time I met Billy. He was friendly and outgoing, and got along well with Charlie right away. After thirty minutes or so, we boarded the plane and were on our way to California. The flight was great. We ate and drank all the way, and before we knew it, we were getting off the plane and into a cab. I took off my leather jacket and put on sunglasses. Everything looked so beautiful and clean compared to Cleveland. Palms trees swayed, the sky was deep blue, and the sun was bright as people jogged and rode bicycles. The mountains in the distance made me feel very peaceful.

"We're in paradise," I said to Charlie.

I'd sure like to call this home, I thought to myself.

We got into Laguna Niguel, and the houses and condos were all upscale with perfect landscaping. Big money. I could see why Amil liked the bank here. We drove a little way up a hill and finally arrived at the condo. It was modern, with two bedrooms, a combination dining and living room, and a kitchen with a dishwasher. The air was chilly from air conditioning. I looked out a back window and there was a golf course right behind the building.

Amil had arranged for the condo to be stocked with lunch meat, bread, milk, pop, and beer. We each made a sandwich, got something to drink, then started discussing the score. A little later, Amil took me outside to the condo garage. There was a 1962 four-door Oldsmobile in it, the Joe Blow car his nephew, Harry, had driven in from Ohio. Amil opened the trunk, pulled up the floor, and showed me the false bottom where all the tools were.

The sun was starting to set, and I told Amil I wanted to see the bank. Amil and Charlie and I drove down the hillside, passed a half dozen estates, and turned left into a small shopping plaza with a sign that said "Monarch Bay Plaza." The Pacific Coast Highway ran off to the side. Amil pointed to the right. At one end of the plaza was a bank. The address was Six Monarch Bay—the United California Bank. It was modern-looking with long, steep wooden shingles and an overhang connecting the bank to a drug store. The bank was hidden pretty well from passing cars by an embankment and a wooded area. It was a nice set-up for a burglary. At the other end of the plaza were a restaurant called the Crown House, a supermarket, a couple of other shops, and some new stores that were being built. There was construction equipment and a couple of trailers.

We parked the car and walked around a little. On the left side of the drugstore was a tall redwood fence enclosure. It was where the garbage containers for the bank were kept. The alarm bell was mounted on the back wall of the bank facing the Pacific Coast Highway.

There wasn't much else to see and not much activity in the shopping center, so we went into the supermarket and bought some more food for the condo. While Amil walked back to the car with the groceries, Charlie and I walked past the bank windows and glass doors. The vault was near the front and to the left of the entrance. There were only two customers at the teller windows.

I was a little concerned about the people who lived on the hillside. The houses were only about two hundred yards away, but Amil had said it was pretty dark at night. Next we walked in the drug store. We noticed that the checkout counter was at the common wall right behind the bank vault. Charlie bought some cigarettes, and we went back to the car and talked to Amil.

We drove around to familiarize ourselves with the area, then went back to the condo. We hung around watching TV and munching snacks until it got dark. Then Amil, James, Charlie, and I changed into dark clothes and went out the back patio door. It was warm, the air smelled sweet, and the sky was packed with stars. We walked through the golf course and down the hill. It took about twenty minutes. At the bottom of the hill, we were able to look down on the shopping plaza. Amil was right. It was dark. There were lights in the stores and in the parking lot, but the roof of the bank was very dark.

Then I looked toward the area under construction and something caught my eye. I pointed, and Amil and Charlie saw it, too. Something was flickering in one of the construction trailers.

"It's a television," I said.

"Are you thinking what I'm thinking?" Amil asked me.

"We have to find out," I said.

"I'll go," Charlie said and got up and headed toward the trailer.

Amil and I waited. About five minutes later, we saw someone come out of the trailer. It looked like an older man wearing a uniform. He looked around for a few seconds, then went back in his trailer. Five minutes after that, Charlie came back.

"Yep, security," he said.

"Is he an armed guard?"

"No," Charlie said, grinning. "Just an old watchman. About seventy. Got good hearing, though. I tossed a little pebble at the trailer and he came right out."

"Let's see if he comes back out," Amil said. "Maybe he won't be a problem. His trailer's got to be about a hundred and fifty yards from the bank."

We sat in the woods behind the plaza and chatted. It had been two hours, and the guard hadn't come out. And not one cop had patrolled through the shopping center. When the stores closed and the lot cleared out, we moved in closer to check out the front part of the bank. We inched our way down the hill in the bushes.

There were big pole lights that lit up the back of the building. I thought that might pose a little problem. We hung around there for about a half hour in the shadows as cars flew up and down the highway. We talked a little more about the watchman and decided that Charlie would monitor the trailer during the score. If the guard heard something and came out, we'd tie him up and tape his mouth. Everything looked good, so we decided to call it a night. I was already exhausted from the flight and time change, and the heat and fresh air of the night made me more tired.

When we got back to the condo, we joined the other guys who were watching television. We would be staying in that night. On an out-of-town score, you don't go out socializing and let your face be seen. When something this big goes down, every cop and fed is running around looking for witnesses who might have seen strangers in the area. Then pretty soon they have a sketch of your face in the newspaper and on the news.

The next morning I got up early, made coffee, and sat on the patio reading the Los Angeles Times. The golfers were already out, and the beautiful sun was rising like in a postcard. Breathing the fresh air and being in the sun made me feel so much better and more alive as compared to the shitty weather and dirty streets in Cleveland. I was daydreaming about living in California. I wanted to wake up in the morning and have breakfast outside while looking at the mountains or ocean. It was a dream, but I was going to make it a reality in my life.

One by one, the rest of the guys got up and had coffee. James volunteered to be the cook for the morning. He fried up some bacon and eggs. I gave him a hand and made toast and got the plates and silverware out. As we ate, we talked about what else had to be done for the score. The only other thing we needed was a ladder to get on the roof of the bank. From the ground to the rooftop was about eighteen feet. I told the guys that there could be a ladder in one of the garages on the hill. We decided to look for one that night when we went down to check the area again for police patrols.

Later in the morning, Amil and I rode by the bank to see how things looked. There were landscapers taking care of the beautiful grass, bushes, and small trees, and inside the bank there were a few customers. Then we went back to the condo and sat around until night. That's when Amil, Charlie, and I walked back down the hill and across the golf course to check out the bank. It was another picturesque night with lots of stars, and unbelievably quiet and peaceful. All I could hear was the chirping of crickets and the fast rhythm of the automatic sprinklers in the background. On our way to the shopping center, we walked a lot closer to the garages of the houses to find a ladder. We kept on checking until we came to a church where we found a big single-section aluminum ladder. We left it, figuring it would be there tomorrow, and continued down the hill to the bank to check things out. Everything looked good except for the watchman in the trailer.

We went back to the condo I started watching TV, but I was too restless. I felt like doing some jogging to make myself tired. The guys thought I was crazy, but I went out the patio door and jogged on the golf course for about a half hour, then walked for a while to cool down. I went back, took a shower, and stretched out on the floor with a pillow under my head. I fell asleep watching a late movie.

The next morning the weather was beautiful again, but my mind was on the score because tonight was the night. A couple of the other guys went out, and James and Charlie took a ride to the supermarket. I didn't want to leave the condo since I was on probation from the pharmaceutical truck break-in and not supposed to leave Ohio. The day went by slowly as I cleaned and checked all of my equipment and waited for the sun to set.

Chapter Fourteen

Finally it got dark. James and Charlie went to the garage, unloaded the other equipment from the Joe Blow car, and brought it inside. We put everything on the floor and checked it. We tested the police scanner and made sure the walkie-talkies worked. They used a special prohibited frequency, so it would be unlikely that anyone was listening in. Harry would monitor the scanner from inside the condo, then warn us on the walkie-talkie if he heard anything. Then he could get the car out of the garage and drive down to pick us up. He wasn't supposed to be driving around unless we needed him because he might draw attention.

We had numerous bags of tools and equipment. In one duffel bag, there were four sticks of dynamite and blasting caps that Amil got. I had my alarm equipment in another duffel bag. There was smaller one that held most of the "in-tools," those needed just to break in. We had a wood drill, key-hole saw, crow-bars, and some screwdrivers. In a long, Army-style bag, we had the lead sledge-hammer, a bunch of empty twenty-five-pound potato bags, and some rope. The bags would be filled with dirt to muffle the sound of the blast. Finally we had brown cotton gloves we would wear to avoid leaving fingerprints.

In another bag we had a custom-made drill. The motor, from a big stand-up fan, ran at twenty-five hundred RPMs, which was especially fast for a drill. It had a special one-inch carbide bit that would pulverize the concrete vault. There were large handles welded on to hold the drill firmly. Then we had a contraption with bottles that looked like thermoses attached to some rubber tubing. It was to shoot liquid Styrofoam into the alarm bell box on the outside of the bank. It would freeze everything solid so that the clapper wouldn't be able to hit the bell.

It was around 10:00 p.m., and everybody except Harry had on dark clothing and gloves. Everyone took a bag or two of tools. I grabbed my bag and the dynamite and had my binoculars hanging on my neck. We told Harry to turn the lights out and walk onto the patio to make sure nobody was around. He came back in and said it was clear. One by one, we slipped out the door and quickly made our way into the darkness and onto the golf course. I glanced back and saw Harry close the patio door and turn the light back on.

My heart was pounding pretty hard like it usually does when moving on a score. My mind was very alert, and I was totally tuned into the night and our plans as we made our way down the hill. Every minute or so, I would stop and use my binoculars to check each house and make sure nobody was watching us.

When we reached the church, James and I ran over, grabbed the ladder, and brought it back into the shadows of the trees. We continued down the hill overlooking the parking lot. We stopped to take a break from carrying the equipment, and I checked the area again with my binoculars. From where we were, I could see the whole shopping center laid out below. Everything looked clear. The guard was in his trailer watching television.

Amil took out the walkie-talkie and spoke with Harry briefly to make sure it worked, then he gave it to Billy. Billy stayed on the hillside just above the plaza where he could watch for anyone pulling into the parking lot. I gave him my binoculars so he could look around every few minutes. With Billy in position, we grabbed the equipment and made our way down the hill to the far side of the parking lot.

We stopped alongside the building and decided that only Amil, James, and I would go on the roof to make entry. Charlie would stay on the ground to help with equipment and keep an eye on the guard. I just hoped he didn't lose his cool and shoot the old guy if he started walking toward the bank.

James and I put the ladder against the side of the building. It was just high enough. We grabbed some small bags of tools. I had my alarm equipment, Amil had a walkie-talkie, and James had the in-tools. The three of us ran up the ladder fast and climbed onto the roof. I looked down and watched as Charlie took the ladder back down, put it out of sight, and disappeared behind some bushes.

Amil, James, and I walked across the roof, over the drugstore, and past a big air conditioning unit until we were on top of the bank. I looked up at the houses on the hill and could see them plainly. I tried to see where Billy was, but it was too dark. After several minutes we located the spot that we figured would be directly above the vault.

James opened the bag of in-tools and took out an L-bar. He scraped away the small stones, then dug into the tar paper and pulled it loose from the wooden roof. When he reached the wood, I drilled a hole. James took the keyhole saw, put it through the hole, and started sawing. While he was cutting, I drilled three more holes to form a square about thirty inches wide. James took a break and Amil finished sawing, connecting the holes. Then James took the pry bar and popped up the section of roof, holding it so it didn't fall in. I grabbed a flashlight and lay on my belly right next to the hole. I stuck the flashlight inside before I turned it on so I didn't light up the roof.

Amil and I went in while James stayed on the roof. I put my ski mask on in case the alarm went off and cameras started taking pictures. We eased onto the top of the bank vault, stepping gently in case there were sound or motion detectors.

We walked very slowly and very quietly across the bank vault ceiling and over to a ladder that led down into the bank. I went first and Amil followed. I was already soaking wet with sweat. We looked around for a second trying to figure out where the telephone wires for the alarm would be. We got down low and made our way behind the counters.

Just off the teller area, we found a small utility room with the phone box. There were about forty or fifty terminals. I put my bag down, took out my meter, and started checking for the alarm. Amil watched as one by one, I carefully checked each terminal. But I couldn't find the alarm. I went through each of the terminals again but still could not find the alarm.

I whispered to Amil that I couldn't believe they didn't have the alarm in here. I told him that I ran into a situation like this before and I had located the alarm wires in a conduit, separate from the phone box. We looked around in the room to see if we could find some conduit, wires, or anything out of place. But there was nothing at all. At this point we had been in the bank for about an hour. Amil wanted to check the phone box himself, so he took my meter and checked each terminal. But he came up with the same thing. No alarm. There wasn't anything left to do, so I put my meter away.

We went back to the ladder and had started toward the top of the vault when we noticed a length of one-and-a-half inch metal conduit that ran alongside, then into the vault. We carefully cut into the conduit with a hacksaw and pipe cutter, but there was only AC power wiring inside.

Amil and I climbed out onto the roof and put the wood piece back. James had a little can of tar and used it to do a quick patch job to camouflage the roof. He had a little mirror that he stuck in the tar, positioning it to reflect the sun if we checked it from the top of the hill with binoculars. We gathered our bags and walked across to where we had come up. I called for Charlie, and he came running with the ladder and placed it against the building. Amil, James, and I quickly made it down to the ground. I told Charlie that we couldn't find the alarm wires. At first he thought I was joking, then realized I was serious. We hid the ladder in the deep bush.

While we were making our way up the hill, Amil called Billy on the walkie-talkie and told him we were coming his way. We got to his position and took a rest. Nobody said a word as we looked down at the bank.

After we rested a minute, we walked up the hill back toward the condo. As we got close, Amil called Harry to let him know we were coming back. I could see the light turn off in the condo. When we were inside, Harry turned the light back on, and all of us dropped our bags of equipment and plopped down wherever we could find a place to sit. We looked like soldiers who just lost a battle. I was hot and thirsty and went to the refrigerator to get a bottle of Pepsi. A couple of the guys got pop and others got beer.

We sat around trying to figure out what to do next. Charlie thought that Amil and I didn't check the alarm right.

"Where the fuck are the alarm wires?" I said.

"Maybe they're in the drugstore," Amil said.

"Maybe you missed a terminal," Charlie suggested.

"The drugstore has an alarm," I said. "But they're open seven days a week. That limits us breaking in to see if the alarm wires are in there. It wouldn't be enough time to complete the bank vault. We'd have to be Superman."

"Are you guys sure you didn't miss a terminal?" Charlie said.

I ignored Charlie. I knew we didn't miss a terminal because Amil and I checked each one three times. But Charlie kept suggesting we didn't check the phone lines good enough. I was getting annoyed, so I told the guys I was going to take a walk. It was about two thirty in the morning. There was no breeze, and the crickets were loud. I started walking, and after a few minutes, my eyes adjusted to the darkness. I was walking for about ten minutes when I decided to jog. It felt good as I ran through the greens of the golf course. My mind was racing about the alarm. I thought of so many possible things, then it hit me. A closed circuit. When I tested the phone terminals, I didn't check for that type of circuit because it was so outdated. It didn't occur to me that a bank would still use it.

I turned around and ran all the way back to the condo. I was sweating and breathing fast when I burst through the door. Everyone was looking at me, wondering what was going on. I turned to Amil.

"I got it. We didn't check for a closed circuit. It's the old way security companies used to wire their alarms. It's so simple to beat. You just short it out. You don't even need an alarm box."

"We've got to check it out," Charlie said.

"It's too late to go back now," I said.

"Yeah, in a few more hours, it'll be getting light," Amil added.

We agreed to move on the bank again the next night. I took a shower, then got a pillow from the bed and stretched out on the floor again. I fell asleep watching TV.

Chapter Fifteen

It was another beautiful California day when I woke up. Sunny. Temperature just right. Fresh-smelling air. We sat around the condo eating and watching TV. Every couple of hours or so, one or two of the guys got in the car and took a ride to the bank to see if there was any commotion. If somebody went on the roof, they might find the hole even though it was patched. So we used the binoculars to make sure the little mirror was still visible. By the time it was getting dark outside, there had been no problems at the bank.

After it got dark, we started getting ready again. I was anxious to find out if my theory was right. We left, and about a half hour later, we were back on the bank roof.

Amil and James and I walked carefully toward the hole. We sure didn't want to fall through. James found the hole, took out a big screwdriver, and pried the wood up. I eased my way in, turned my flashlight on, and glanced around. Then I heard Billy say something over Amil's walkie-talkie. Instantly my heart was pounding fast and hard.

I popped my head out of the hole and asked what was going on. Amil motioned for me to be quiet and said softly that people were coming out of the supermarket and that it looked like employees leaving for the night. I climbed out of the hole and waited until Billy said that they were gone. I climbed back into the hole and Amil followed. We moved right to the ladder, down into the bank, and directly to the room with the phone box like we owned the place. I set my meter and started checking each terminal. I went through the first dozen or so and thought I might be wrong. Maybe the alarm wires were hidden. I didn't know what we would do in that case because we didn't discuss it. I kept checking terminals and still couldn't find the alarm. I only had about twenty to go.

"Bingo," I whispered to Amil as I got a proper reading across the terminals. I double-checked and knew I had it. Amil and I smiled at each other. Now we had to knock out the outside bell first, because it could still activate if we set off a sensor alarm in the vault. The alarm wouldn't show in the police station or at an alarm company, but the bell would go off and make a racket.

We went back up to the roof and told James we found the alarm. Then the three of us walked across the roof along the side of the building. I whistled once, and Charlie poked his head out of the bushes. I motioned for him to bring the ladder, and he came running, struggling a bit as the ladder banged loudly against the wall. Amil, James, and I slid down and hurried out of sight. When we got around to the side by the bell, we could hear cars and trucks going up and down the highway.

The big lights in the parking lot sure were bright. And the area by the bell was only partially hidden by trees. We were concerned that we might be seen by someone passing by on the highway, which was only seventy-five feet away. I told Amil we should knock out the one light on the side by the bell. It would be a lot darker, but nobody would notice one light out. Amil said that was a good idea. James and Charlie knew what we were going to do and just waited. Amil and I got a screwdriver and wire cutters out of my bag and ran over to the base of the light pole. We sure didn't like being in the light, so we worked fast. There was a metal plate with four screws at the bottom of the light pole. I took one of them out, loosened the others, and flipped the plate up so I could see inside where the wires were. Amil had the wire cutters in his hand. I carefully reached inside and pulled the wires out. Amil cut one wire, and the light went out. It made a big difference in the main spot we would be working in.

James and Amil said they would knock out the bell. Amil grabbed the two small containers that looked like thermoses. When James got up the ladder to the bell, he whispered down that it was a Diebold. Diebold was originally a safe company that got into other parts of the security industry later. Their alarm bell box had an alarm trip on one of the bolts. If the wrong bolt was removed, the alarm would go off. I told James which was the right one to remove, and he started turning it with a wrench. He almost had it out, then started turning it by hand very slowly. It seemed like it was taking forever. Finally the bolt came out, and there was no alarm.

Amil handed the two canisters to his brother, and James took the tube and stuck one end of it in the hole where the bolt had been. He pushed the button and started filling the bell box with liquid Styrofoam.

As I turned to check the highway, I heard Amil say, "That's enough. It's coming down the wall."

There wasn't a lot, but it had to be wiped off quickly before it hardened fast. We didn't want the law to happen by and see white liquid Styrofoam dripping down from the bell box. James handed the canisters back to Amil, then took off his T-shirt right away and wiped the wall down as best he could.

Now that we knocked out the bell, we were ready to go back in the bank and jump out the alarm. Amil and I took the ladder to the other side of the building, and we climbed up fast. James and Charlie stayed on the ground.

Amil and I put on our ski masks again and climbed back through the hole and into the bank. We went right to the phone terminal box and jumped out the alarm. Then we hurried back up to the roof, slid down the ladder, and hid in the bushes. We waited about thirty minutes. There was no bell, no police cars, and no call on the walkie-talkie from Harry.

I grabbed the ladder, and we ran to the side of the building. Amil took the bag with the dynamite and blasting caps, and another small bag of tools, and

James grabbed a bag with the drill and rope in it. Charlie kept watch as I placed the ladder against the wall and the Dinsios scooted up. Then I moved the ladder back to the cover of the bushes and trees.

Billy took over watching the guard's trailer, while Charlie and I started taking turns shoveling dirt and holding the bags open. I tied them, one at a time, onto the rope, and James pulled them up to the roof. I kept on fastening them onto the rope while Charlie was filling the bags quick and tying the ends closed. My heart was pounding hard and I was starting to slow down, but I kept working quickly.

"That should be enough," James said.

We were supposed to fill all twenty bags, but we only did about twelve because they were fuller and heavier than we thought they'd be. I stepped back behind the trees to catch my breath. After resting a minute, I grabbed the sledgehammer and other heavy tools, and joined the Dinsios on the roof. Charlie took the ladder down and disappeared into the darkness.

Amil and James had already moved the bags over to the hole. It was sure good to be on a score with them because they did a lot of the work. James eased down on top of the vault, and I handed him the drill, then looked for a place to plug it in. There were electrical boxes and the air conditioning unit on the roof, but no outlet. Amil said he'd splice into the AC. I gave him a pair of wire cutters, a screwdriver, and some black tape.

James was ready to go. All he needed was power. I looked at Amil to see if he was having problems, but he was doing fine. For a moment we were at a standstill as I looked around and up at the houses in the area. I could hear the traffic on the freeway but couldn't see it from where I was. Otherwise everything was quiet. I could smell the roof tar, which was still warm from the heat of the day.

When Amil finished the splice, we hung a work light into the opening. Then James drilled one hole about ten inches deep, almost the length of the bit. The drill was so powerful that it ate right through the concrete. James continued to drill more holes, moving in a big circle.

When James finished, he had about nine holes in a circle about three feet in diameter, with one in the middle. He put the drill down and said he needed something to clear the concrete dust out of the holes. I gave him the cutting torch with the oxygen and acetylene tanks. He turned the knob on the oxygen bottle, and it started hissing while he blew the dust out of the holes.

I grabbed the duffel bag with the dynamite and blasting caps and jumped down into the hole with James. He took out one stick of dynamite, and I got another one. We used razor knives to cut three-inch pieces of dynamite. Then we stuck the blasting caps in and pushed one piece of dynamite into each hole. We used the handle of a screwdriver to nudge them down.

When we were finished, we paired up all the wires and pulled them to one side. Amil disconnected the electrical splice, then handed us the dirt bags one by one. We piled them all around, on top of the vault ceiling and the dynamite. Then we brought all the tools out of the hole.

I picked up the wires from the dynamite, and James had the extension cord from the drill. I asked Amil if he was sure the wires were off the power lines, and he said yes. We connected the dynamite wires to the extension cord, crawled out of the hole, and moved back about thirty feet.

Amil looked at me. I knew what he was thinking. We were experienced with explosives but weren't absolutely sure how loud the blast would be. I looked around for Charlie and could see that he was watching the guard trailer closely. He had his pistol in one hand and a cigarette in the other. I nodded to Amil. He took the other end of the extension cord and touched the bare ends against the electrical lines. There was a little thud, then silence. The bags were very effective in muffling the blast. They also helped to direct the blast downward into the vault ceiling. Some dust and smoke was rising from the hole.

James and I ran to the hole and looked in. The dirt bags were thrown around just a little, but the whole inside was filled with smoke and dust. The shockwave had blown out the bulb in our work light. We were hoping that we'd used enough dynamite and wouldn't have to drill and blast again. I held the flashlight in my hand as James moved some of the bags out of the way. I could see a lot of busted-up concrete, but it didn't look like the one blast had been enough.

James got more of the bags out of the way, then moved some of the bigger chunks of concrete. It looked like more of the vault ceiling had been blown away than I first thought. After some of the dust cleared out, James gave the concrete a couple of good shots with the ten-pound hammer. It hardly made any noise when it hit, but a good portion broke loose from the reinforcing rods and fell in. He gave it another whack, and a big part of the vault ceiling fell in. There was still enough left for us to stand on and work.

We peered in, and our flashlights reflected off the shiny wall of safe-deposit boxes. All we had to do was cut the reinforcing bars with the acetylene torch. While James finished clearing away the concrete, I walked over to the side where Charlie was. I got to the edge of the building and whistled once.

Charlie ran over and said, "What's up?"

"We're in."

"When are you going to blow?"

"We already did. We're in."

"You mean you're in the vault? I didn't hear a thing." Charlie said. He was pacing back and forth like a kid who couldn't wait for Christmas.

I laughed to myself. Charlie would get so excited on scores. "Yeah, yeah," I said. "We're in."

He went back to watch the guard's trailer, and I moved the acetylene and oxygen tanks close to the roof hole. Then James came out and I went in, and he helped me put the tanks on top of the vault. I adjusted them, lit the torch, and started burning the rebar. There were about eight rods, roughly three-quarters of an inch thick. The molten metal was falling onto the vault floor and burning the tile. Between the dust from the blast and smoke from the torch, I was coughing a lot.

As I cut each rod, James grabbed it before it fell into the vault. After I finished burning all the rods, I gathered the torch, hose, and tanks. By this time the whole area was filled with smoke, and it was very hard to breathe.

"We better take a break until the smoke clears out," I said.

We gathered all the equipment we didn't need inside and brought it to the side of the building where we'd come up. After we stood there for a while, Charlie whispered up to us.

"I want to come up."

"Okay, we can use some extra help up here."

Charlie came running toward us with the ladder, threw it against the wall, and hurried up to the roof, and we pulled the ladder up. I told Charlie we were waiting for all the smoke in the vault to clear. He was still saying he couldn't believe we were inside the vault because he didn't hear any noise at all from the dynamite. About ten minutes went by, and I kneeled down and looked into the hole with the flashlight. The smoke had cleared and I could see inside.

"It's show time," I said.

Chapter Sixteen

Amil, James, Charlie, and I climbed down into the vault. I could still smell the tile smoldering. We found the light switch, turned it on, and looked around. There had to be five hundred safe-deposit boxes in the vault, which was about twelve feet by fifteen feet. In a little attached room, there were two small safes that I knew would be simple to open.

James and Charlie went into the other room to work on the small safes while Amil and I started working on the safe-deposit boxes. Each box had one lock with two keyholes, one for the bank employee's key and the other for the box holder's key. But Amil and I were getting into the boxes a different way. While I was swinging the sledgehammer, Amil was holding another hammer that's used for knocking rivets out of big metal beams. The hammer has a wooden handle and a point on one side of the head, which was ground down smaller to fit the keyhole. The other side is flat so when you hit it with the lead sledgehammer, it doesn't glance off or make a loud noise.

Amil and I hammered away at the boxes while the sweat was rolling down our faces. Sometimes we could pop the lock with one good swing, though usually it would take two. We had to take breaks now and then and switch off swinging the sledgehammer.

After we opened about ten boxes, we stopped, opened the doors, pulled out the boxes and looked inside before we dumped the contents into the big cloth bags we had. We were getting jewelry, cash, and a lot of bearer bonds, which we knew could be cashed easily.

In the meantime James and Charlie cleared out the small safes, which only contained about fifty-five thousand dollars in cash. Then they came into the vault and helped us. Amil and I would get the doors open, and James and Charlie would empty the boxes into the bags. There was a lot of jewelry, gold coins, and cash as we continued going down the lines of boxes.

As things started getting cluttered in the vault, we threw the empty boxes and worthless items in the other room. I couldn't believe what some people put in these boxes. We found baby shoes. We found false teeth. But that wasn't the strangest thing we found.

James said, "Look at this, Phil."

He handed me a metal box. There was writing on top, and I realized it contained the ashes of a dead person. I used both hands and gave it back to James.

"Put it back where you found it," I told him.

I surely didn't want to disturb the ashes of a dead person.

Suddenly Billy called on the walkie-talkie.

"A car just pulled into the parking lot in the front of the bank," he said.

We froze and stared at the walkie-talkie. Amil held it up to his mouth and asked Billy what the person was doing.

Billy said, "He turned his lights off. It's a man and he's just sitting there."

We couldn't figure out what was going on. Billy came back over the radio. His voice was a little shaky. "He's getting out of the car and walking toward the bank door. He's opening the bank door."

I whispered to Amil that maybe it was a cleaning person. He agreed that it probably was. We all stood very still trying to hear the guy come into the bank lobby. We were being as quiet as possible. We could hear him moving around but couldn't tell what he was doing.

Suddenly Charlie started coughing. He always coughed because he smoked too much, and the dust from when we blew the vault probably wasn't helping. We all motioned to Charlie to stop coughing and keep quiet. We continued to listen. Billy said he couldn't see him from where he was.

We were all standing very still and straining to hear, when Charlie started coughing again. We looked at him in disbelief. He was hacking away and not covering his mouth. I whispered to him to go up on the roof and pointed up the hole. I know we were all thinking that if this guy hears Charlie coughing, he'll call the police and we'll have to run out of there fast.

Then Charlie started to cough again. I put my hand over his mouth and said, "Get up on the fuckin' roof."

I removed my hand as he put his hand over his mouth. He continued coughing as he climbed the ladder and went onto the roof.

Amil whispered into the walkie-talkie, asking Billy if he could see anything. Billy answered that he had seen the man moving around but couldn't see him now. Thank God we got Charlie out of there and onto the roof. We could hear the muffled sound of him coughing with his hand over his mouth.

Amil handed the radio to James and put his ear close to the vault door, listening. I heard Charlie cough again and shook my head. I looked up the hole and could see him looking down.

I motioned him back and whispered, "Get the fuck away from the hole."

Then I saw him move away.

Now it was very quiet inside the vault, and we couldn't hear anything. We were whispering to each other. We didn't know if this guy heard Charlie coughing and called the law. I thought we should all go up on the roof until we knew everything was all right. But then we heard a noise in the bank office. Then we heard more noises like the guy was moving something around. We figured he didn't hear anything, or it would have been quiet.

A call came over the walkie-talkie. James had the volume down low and the microphone to his ear. Billy wanted to know if Harry should get in the car and stand by in case of any problems. It was impossible for James to reply from inside the vault because he'd have to talk too softly. I whispered in James's ear that he should go on the roof to talk to answer Billy. James went up the step ladder very quietly and onto the roof.

About a half hour went by, but it seemed like forever as Amil and I sat there in the vault. Finally James came down and said the guy was gone.

"Well, it was a nice break. Let's get back to work," I said.

Amil and I started working again and were soon sweating like pigs. James helped bag the papers, stocks, bearer bonds, and whatever else was valuable.

Charlie never came back. He just stood on the roof. We really didn't need him down there, and he knew we were pissed at him for coughing.

It was about an hour before dawn when we finished with the boxes. We didn't get all of the boxes open, but we had most of them. We bagged everything up and got ready to leave. While James and I were moving the loot toward the ladder, Amil went back to the door of the vault with a big screwdriver and damaged the locking mechanism timer.

James went up the ladder to the top of the vault. I handed him all the bags, and he gave them to Charlie on the roof. Before I knew it, everything was on the roof, and I was climbing out of the hole. The cool fresh air of the early morning felt like heaven because I was still hot and sweaty.

Amil came out last and we were ready to leave, but we still had a lot of bags to gather. We moved our bags of tools, the stocks and bonds, money, jewelry, and gold coins toward the side of the roof. Charlie and I climbed down to the ground. Amil and James threw all the bags down to us, except the ones with the big, heavy tools and the leftover dynamite. One by one, the guys came off the side of the roof, bringing the heavy bags down. When they got close, I would grab them. Soon we had everything off the roof.

We started moving everything, including the ladder, out of sight and into the underbrush. So far everything was going great. But we knew we had to get moving because it would be light very soon. Without saying anything, I grabbed two of the biggest bags and started walking up the incline to the top where Billy was. I was moving hard and fast, and when the others saw me, they grabbed everything else and followed me. I felt like a pack mule going up the hill. When I got to Billy, I dropped the bags. My eyes were burning from sweat, my heart was pounding, and I was exhausted.

I took a break until the others caught up. When they all got to the top, I picked up my bags and started moving through the golf course toward the condo. I could hear the others behind me. When I got about fifty yards from the condo, I stopped again to wait for the others. We would have to call Harry in the condo to turn off the lights and open the patio doors. When the others caught up, Billy called Harry on the radio, and instantly the lights went off. All of the lights in the other condos were off, too. We all made it into the condo, and Harry put the lights back on. The air conditioning was on, and it was very cool. I just fell on the couch with exhaustion, and before I knew it, the sun started lighting the sky. We couldn't have planned it any closer. We sat around for a little while talking about different things and especially about Charlie coughing, which Harry and Billy didn't know about. But it was over, and we laughed about it now.

Amil dumped the big bags on the floor, and we started going through them. It was breathtaking to see the value of the bearer bonds because they totaled at least $20 million. We were smiling and laughing because we knew we were rich. We sorted everything into piles but weren't going to cut up anything there. That would be done back home. James had bought a speedboat in California and was going to trailer it, with the loot inside, back to Ohio.

Charlie said, "Did you guys get all of the safe boxes?"

"No," I said. "Almost all of them."

"Are you going to go back and get the rest?" he asked.

"I don't think it would be worth it."

James and Amil agreed.

"We've pushed our luck far enough," I added. "I'm tired and want to get the farthest away from here as I can get. And the sooner the better."

Everybody agreed. We put everything in separate bags and laid them aside. I took a shower, went to bed, and fell asleep immediately. The next morning I woke up early and before anybody else. It was about six thirty, and you could tell it was going to be another beautiful California day. I sure liked California but wanted to get back home before the burglary was discovered.

I kept thinking about all the bearer bonds we had. If we could get rid of them, we would all clear about $1 million apiece. This is what it was all about: make the big score, be rich, and be somebody instead of a neighborhood bum.

I kept on daydreaming while I made some coffee. One by one, everybody started getting up.

"Can you imagine Monday when they go to open the vault door," I said, "and it won't open because we screwed up the timing mechanism on the clock? Then when they do get inside and find out they were robbed, this place will be swarming with FBI agents."

"And that old guard is gonna shit when he finds out what he missed," Charlie said.

We all roared with laughter. Later, Charlie and I called the airline from a payphone and made reservations for later that afternoon. Harry drove us to the airport, and before we knew it, we were flying back to Cleveland. Charlie and I had a drink and saluted our good fortune.

When we arrived in Cleveland, it was cold and dirty. I knew someday I would move out of Cleveland to where it was warm and clean.

I went right to the Redwood to see how things were going. Everything looked good, so I went home to see Maggie. She told me a lot of guys had been calling, looking for me. Everything seemed the same as when I left. I was tired and needed some sleep.

The next morning, I got up early like I always did—just me, the birds, my newspaper, and coffee. But I couldn't get my mind off the score we had just pulled off.

Chapter Seventeen

FBI SPECIAL AGENT (RET.) FRANK CALLEY: I was assigned to assist Special Agent Jim Conway, of the Santa Ana Resident Agency, with a bank burglary. It was located in a shopping plaza across from the Monarch Beach portion of Laguna Niguel, in Orange County, in a hilly area right on the ocean.

When I got to the vault, I couldn't believe what a mess it was. There was debris and white dust all over from where the burglars had blasted in. Almost all of the five hundred or so safe-deposit boxes were broken into, and leftover contents scattered around, including birth certificates, marriage licenses, divorce papers, death certificates, insurance policies, military decorations, and photographs. There were also several half-gallon milk containers filled with water that the burglars had used either for drinking or for cooling down their cutting tools. The burglars were obviously professionals because they had left behind a pile of non-negotiable bonds that would be impossible to fence.

Over several days we searched the scene and photographed each piece of evidence. Orange County Sheriff's Office detectives and crime scene techs did a good job processing the crime scene. We found hundreds of pieces—chisels and other hand tools, tape, wire, batteries—then removed them to the Sheriff's Office headquarters. Each piece of evidence was then examined and catalogued.

This was an unusual case for Southern California. We had plenty of bank robberies, but no bank burglaries. And so we started reviewing old files from some bank burglaries that had occurred in other parts of the United States. The files showed similarly styled burglaries in Georgia, Florida, and Missouri, in which Cleveland and Youngstown individuals, including James and Amil Dinsio and Phil Christopher, were suspects.

Now that we had some names to work with, we started hitting hotels in Los Angeles and Orange County to see if we could find any record of the suspects having visited Southern California. Agents from other squads were assigned temporarily to help, but we came up with nothing.

PHIL: About a week after we got back from California, Amil called me from Youngstown. He told me to stop over in a few days. I knew that meant James had got back okay, and it was time to split up the loot.

There wasn't anything in the Cleveland newspapers, but I did notice quite a few cars tailing me lately. Then a guy I knew from down the street told me it looked like some guys were watching my place from where they were parked in front of his house. I told him I couldn't imagine why they would be watching me. I didn't want him to know I was concerned because he was a half-ass burglar who knew some of the same people I knew. And I didn't want anyone to know I was involved in the California score. I figured the cars were just Cleveland detectives like James Sweeney or Rocco Poluttro, who were always keeping tabs on us.

The next day Ray Ferritto called.

"Where ya been?" he said.

Before I could say I was in Canada, he asked, "Were you in California?"

Ray caught me off guard, but I played it off and laughed.

"I wish I was vacationing in California, but I was in Canada, bear hunting."

He didn't say anything for a few seconds.

"Are you going up to see Ronnie?" he said.

"Yeah, probably in a day or so."

Then Ray said that he was in Youngstown. I thought he was in Erie, Pennsylvania, when he called. We said goodbye, and I was trying to figure out what that was all about. He must have heard about the score from one of the guys in California and was pissed that he was left out.

Then I got a call from Charlie. He asked if I was going to be home. He often called to ask if I was home then would stop over. But this time he must have been right around the corner because he pulled in my driveway just a minute or so after we hung up.

When I went to the side door and let him in, Charlie looked a little excited.

"Phil, I've been tailed all day."

I didn't find that odd because every now and then, the local detectives followed him around. Charlie was also paranoid.

"So what? You've been tailed before."

"Yeah, but these aren't normal detective cars. I think they're the feds."

"That's impossible. You're paranoid."

I told Charlie I'd meet him at the Redwood the next day, and we'd go see Amil. The next morning we left for Youngstown. Charlie drove. He always liked to drive. I brought my binoculars with me and kept checking behind as we headed down Interstate 271 toward the Ohio Turnpike. I told Charlie to take a secondary road so that the toll booth attendants wouldn't recognize us from the pictures the police gave them to keep tabs on us. We made it all the way to Youngstown with no problem, parked in Amil's driveway, and went into the house. We sat in Amil's kitchen and talked to his wife for a few minutes, then Amil came in and we went downstairs. His brother James came in about five minutes later.

First Amil brought out the bag with the fifty-five thousand dollars in cash from the small safes. After we split up the cash, we brought out the diamonds and jewelry. Some were so big they looked like costume jewelry. We started picking out what we liked and tried to split things up evenly. I picked out several pieces I thought Maggie would like. We decided to send the rest to a fence and split the money later.

Then we went through the gold coins. Some were in tubes. Most were South African Krugerrands. I didn't know much about gold, so I let the other guys do the dealing about what was what. After the gold was split evenly, I asked Amil about Harry's and Billy's cut. He said he'd take care of them.

Charlie brought up the bearer bonds. James and Amil said they added up to a little over $20 million, but they thought we might only get twenty-five cents on the dollar for them. Charlie thought he could get fifty cents on the dollar. I just listened because I had never dealt with bonds before. I liked cash or diamonds. Charlie and I took one hundred thousand dollars worth of bonds to start with. Amil said he would hold the rest.

After we were done, I told Amil we were going into town to see Ronnie Crab. Charlie and I drove into Youngstown, but nobody was around. We made a few calls but couldn't find anyone. I thought it was just as well because I didn't feel like getting the third degree about where I had been, although it was nobody's business anyway.

As Charlie and I headed back to Cleveland, we discussed fencing the bonds. Charlie said he thought Shondor Birns could move them for us. Shondor was a well-known Jewish racketeer with connections to the Mafia. He was about sixty-five years old or so. I'd never had any dealings with him, but I thought if we could get fifty cents on the dollar, I didn't care who we fenced them off to.

In the meantime, I hid the bonds in my brother's basement. Charlie didn't want to take them home, and I surely didn't want to bring them in my house. I wasn't scared to take the cash home because Amil had already got it changed with Pat Ferruccio, his guy in Canton, Ohio. Pat was an old-timer who was well-connected to the Pittsburgh Mafia.

The next day Charlie and I drove downtown to the Theatrical Bar and Grill to meet Shondor Birns. The Theatrical had a cozy atmosphere with tables all around the oval-shaped bar and an elevated platform in the middle where bands performed.

There were a lot of people eating lunch there that day. I saw several people I knew—a few attorneys, a couple of bookmakers, and a few assholes who thought they were gangsters. But most of them were just parasites. I started thinking that maybe I shouldn't have come along. These people would know I was up to something because I was never at the Theatrical during the day. Once in a while, I'd go at night. I didn't care for the people who hung around there, but I did love their prime rib every now and then.

As Charlie and I sat at the bar, I noticed a lot of eyes looking at me, but I played it off. I was just there to get a quick sandwich and would be gone. Then I heard Charlie say hello to Shondor Birns. I looked, and Shondor was sitting a few barstools away from us.

Shondor yelled, "Hello, Charlie!"

I thought to myself, what is this guy, an asshole or what? Can he talk any louder? Charlie got up and walked over to him, then they both went to the back of the restaurant towards the men's room. Charlie motioned for me to come, but I waved him off. A lot of people were watching Charlie and Shondor as they went into the men's room.

The bartender brought my sandwich and Coke. I ate fast, and by time I was done, Charlie and Shondor walked back to the bar and stopped behind me. Charlie introduced us. I turned around, said hi to Shondor, and we shook hands.

He said to me loudly, "I hear you're doing pretty good."

I smiled but was thinking to myself, what an obnoxious asshole.

I said, "I'm keeping my head above water."

Shondor just laughed. I'm glad he didn't say anything more to me. Charlie told him we'd see him later. They shook hands, and Shondor walked back to where he had been sitting. Charlie sat down to eat his sandwich.

Shondor yelled to him, "I'll see you later with those things."

I was pissed now. I said to Charlie, "Is this mother-fucker nuts?"

"Nobody knows what we're talking about, Phil."

"Let's get the fuck outta here. I'm going to pay the check and I'll be outside."

I got up and was purposely looking at the check as I passed Shondor's table. I didn't want to have any more contact with him.

But he noticed me and said, "See you later."

I looked up like I was surprised and said, "Oh yeah, I'll see you."

I couldn't get out of there any faster. We were walking to the car and I said to Charlie, "Is that guy a fucking idiot? Does he think he has a license to do things illegally?"

Charlie said, "That's just the way he is, Phil. He's loud, but he's got a lotta connections."

"Well I don't like being around him. Keep me out of it."

"I'll meet him tonight alone and bring him the bonds. He said he can move 'em with no problem."

"Good. I just don't like his big mouth."

Chapter Eighteen

The Redwood had become more trouble than it was worth, so I sold it. I put the money on the street in a "shylock," a loan operation with a friend. He was very good with money because, ironically, he was an accountant.

The Redwood continued to be a popular spot, and I still hung out there with my crew for fun. Every now and then, we'd see undercover cops doing surveillance on the bar. I heard that one of them remarked that if the walls in the Redwood could talk, they could solve most of the burglaries in town—and some of the murders.

Despite our success with the United California Bank score, we were a little disappointed that the bank didn't have more hard cash. And so in May, Amil and James Dinsio located a bank in Lordstown, Ohio, where we would try our luck again. The Dinsios said they had inside information that the bank would be loaded with payroll cash for the huge Lordstown General Motors Assembly Plant.

The bank was just outside of Youngstown and off the Ohio Turnpike. It sat real nice, with a dirt road and wooded area nearby. There was one house across the road from the bank, but we didn't think that would pose a problem.

I met the Dinsios at the truck stop off the Ohio Turnpike to discuss the plans. And as a favor to Cleveland Mafia boss Jack Licavoli, it was agreed that Joe Gallo, a mob soldier, would be included. Gallo needed money to pay for a lawyer in a pending drug case. But to balance out the take, James wanted to exclude Charlie. So I told the Dinsios I would split my end with him. They were surprised but said they didn't care if that's how I wanted to do it. Charlie was mad, but I convinced him it was better than nothing.

The day of the score, I picked up my Joe Blow car from the garage of my partner in the shylock business, where I kept it stashed. It was a dark blue, 1968 Buick four-door. The bulb was pulled out of the dome light so it wouldn't light up the interior when the doors opened. Charlie followed me in his car to Youngstown. Every time I got to a toll gate, I put on glasses and a hat so that the toll workers wouldn't recognize me from the photos.

We all met at James's house around 8:00 p.m. There were Amil, James, Charlie, Joe Gallo, Amil's brother-in-law Billy, and myself. The first time I laid eyes on Joe Gallo, he was loading an M-1 carbine that had two long banana clips taped back to back. I thought to myself, I'd never gone on a score where we had that much firepower.

We discussed the score, and it was decided that Billy would drive the Joe Blow car and have the police scanner and a walkie-talkie. He'd drop us off and pick us up. Amil showed me his new jumper box that he was going to use. It had a long cable that you could connect to the alarm wires on a building and run a distance to the jumper box. This would be an additional margin of safety in case the alarm was tripped. He nicknamed it "the Boss."

At about 10:00 p.m., we loaded the tools in the Joe Blow car and left. Everything was quiet as we approached the area of the bank. Billy turned his headlights off just before he turned down the dirt road. When he got to the end of the road, about a half mile from the bank, he stopped. We grabbed our bags of tools and jumped out fast. We left one walkie-talkie with him, and Charlie and I each had one. Billy took off in the car, and we made our way on foot through the high weeds until we came to a group of trees.

My eyes were getting used to the dark now, and I could see that the bank was about two hundred yards away. I could barely see the lights from the house across from the bank. We left the heavy tools by the trees and just brought the jumper box with us. We decided that Amil and James would go on the roof while I stayed with the boss box. Charlie and Joe Gallo would stay by the trees and be lookouts.

I stopped about fifty yards away and held the boss box and one end of the extension wire while Amil and James went across the parking lot and to the bank with the other end. They also had a couple of bags of tools and two big Army duffel bags for the cash. When they reached the building, James cupped his hands together, and Amil stepped up and pulled himself right onto the roof. Then Amil got down on his belly, put one arm over the side of the building, and pulled James up. They looked like acrobats.

About thirty minutes went by, then Amil and James came off the roof in a hurry and ran to where I was.

I called Billy on the walkie-talkie and said, "Listen up."

That was our signal for him to monitor the police scanner and be ready to pick us up if there was a problem. It was only a few seconds later that Billy called and said there was word on the scanner of an alarm at the bank. Amil and James looked at each other and were mad. Something had gone wrong with the jumper box. We backed off and waited by the tree line.

Sure enough, a few minutes later, two Lordstown police cars came flying into the parking lot. They went right under the boss box wire but didn't see it. A minute later, a third officer pulled in. They circled the bank and shined their spotlights in the windows. Charlie and Joe came running up to us with their guns ready. I told them to just relax and wait inside the woods.

The police cars all stopped by the front door, and the cops got out. They looked in the front windows, pulled on the locked door, then went back to their cars. One car left, and the two others parked side by side and just sat there. They were about twenty feet away from the boss box cable. If they saw it, they could follow it right to the boss box. Amil, James, and I backed off to the tree line to give ourselves more time to get away if they saw the wire.

It was very quiet except for a dog that was barking from outside the house across the street from the bank. It must have sensed the commotion of the police checking the alarm. Amil, James, and I talked softly while we watched what the police were doing. We figured they were treating this like a false alarm, but we didn't know how long they'd hang around. I suggested that maybe they were waiting for the bank manager or somebody. We were just hoping they wouldn't see the cable overhead.

We discussed what our options were if the police left. We decided to wait for them to leave, then see if they came back to check on the bank. Forty-five minutes later, one police car left. Ten minutes after that, the other one left. We were on pins and needles, waiting to see if they were going to return and if our score would be ruined. An hour went by, and the police had not come back.

By then it was about one o'clock in the morning. All you could hear were the bugs making noises. Amil and James did their acrobatics getting on the roof with two bags of tools and went back to work. Then the dog across the street started barking again.

About fifteen minutes went by, and Amil and James came off the roof. Amil said they had already made their way inside the bank through an air duct. They said the dog was making them nervous, so they thought they should have the walkie-talkie inside with them. Charlie said that he and Joe Gallo would go quiet the dog down. Charlie pulled out a silencer and screwed it on his pistol. Then off he and Joe went. I could hear the dog barking more and more. Then suddenly it stopped.

As soon as Charlie and Joe got back, Amil called Billy on the walkie-talkie and said, "Hang in tight. We're going to get the groceries."

Amil and James ran back to the bank and were up on roof and out of sight in no time. We had to rush now. Because of the delay with the alarm going off and the police coming, it was soon going to be daylight. Joe Gallo was standing there with his M-1 carbine like he was ready for war.

Before I knew it, Amil and James appeared on the roof again. They dropped the overstuffed Army bags to the ground and they landed with a thud. Then James and Amil jumped down.

They ran to us struggling with the big bags. I peeked in and they were packed with stacks and stacks of cash. We called Billy and told him to pick us up at home, then we moved quickly to where he'd dropped us off. Charlie stayed behind with the walkie-talkie to bring the boss box. When Billy pulled up, we called Charlie and told him to come home. He came running like a bullet after he pulled the box off the telephone wire. We left immediately and kept listening to the police scanner, but no calls of an alarm came over it.

At James's house where we went to cut up the money, James emptied both bags onto a big round table. While we were counting the money, Joe Gallo said to Charlie that he should take lessons on how to shoot a gun. Apparently Charlie had tried to shoot the dog but hit a piece of metal near the dog house instead. The noise of the bullet hitting the metal scared the dog so much that it ran into its house and stopped barking.

The total for the Lordstown bank score was almost a half million dollars. It was an especially nice haul because it was all cash. Nothing would have to be fenced like the bonds from Laguna Niguel.

Phil, age six.

Phil, age nine,
posing in his driveway.

Phil (upper right corner) at age 17, with his parents,
paternal grandparents, and brother at
the grandparents' 50th wedding anniversary.

left: Phil, age 12, recovering from rheumatic fever and displaying "Sea Witch," one of his model boats.

right: Phil in his Collinwood High School graduation photo.

Eugene Ciasullo first taught young Phil how to force open a safe and gave him a set of master keys to steal cars and trucks. In later years he became a well-known Mafia enforcer.

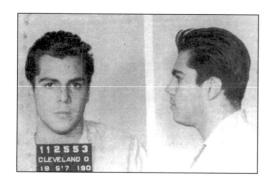 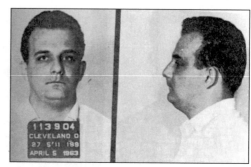

Phil in an early mug shot.

Tommy Teren, one of Phil's criminal associates from Canada.

Phil, right, with former best friend Charlie Broeckel, who turned government informant and falsely implicated him in a murder. Phil was acquitted.

Frank "Skinny" Velotta was close with mob capo Jimmy "the Weasel" Fratianno.

Al Walch recruited Phil into the iron workers' union battle and later relocated to southern California.

Mafia-connected burglars, associates of Phil, who were active in the Los Angeles, California area during the late 1960s and early 1970s

Ray Ferritto, hit man in the Julius Petro murder, was also a principal in the 1977 bombing death of notorious Mafia foe Danny "the Irishman" Greene.

Julius Petro was thought by his fellow California-based burglars and Mafia associates to be a police informant. Phil believed Petro tipped off LAPD in the failed private safe-deposit box company score from which Phil narrowly escaped. Petro was killed in a parking garage at Los Angeles International Airport by Ray Ferritto.

Bob Walsh was an ex-cop-turned-burglar and con man.

Ronnie Carrabbia, Mahoning Valley mob boss during the seventies, and close friend of Phil.

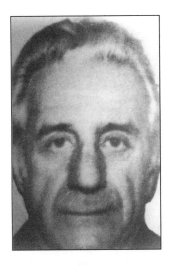

Jimmy "the Weasel" Fratianno, California mob capo for whom Phil planted a bomb at a Los Angeles dry cleaning establishment whose owner Fratianno was trying to shake down.

Brothers Amil and James Dinsio, master burglars from Youngstown, Ohio, and Phil's partners in the Lordstown, Ohio and Orange County, California Bank scores

Rear of United California Bank's Laguna Niguel branch and ladder used by burglars.

Inside of vault showing entry from ceiling.

Inside of vault showing door in background and ransacked safe-deposit boxes in foreground.

Top area of vault showing roof entry (covered by tarp) and leftover dirt-filled bags that were used to muffle the blast.

A wall of mangled safe deposit boxes at the United California Bank.

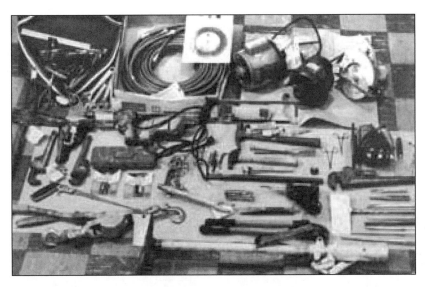

Leftover tools recovered by Orange County Sheriff's Office and FBI crime scene investigators.

It was a different era, in 1972, when Phil was housed in the jail in Mahoning County, Ohio. Mafia influence and corruption ran deep into local government. The following photographs were taken by Phil's girlfriend, Maggie, who occasionally spent a night with him at the jail.

Kicking back in the captain's office...

...and drinking homemade wine in the captain's office.

"Breaking in" to the jail candy machine.

Clowning in the jail shower.

Phil, age 28, in 1971, the same year he was shot at by Albany, New York police officers during a dry run that went bad.

Jack Licavoli, the mob boss whose offer of employment Phil declined.

The murder of persistent Mafia foe Danny "the Irishman" Greene sparked a war between Pittsburgh and Cleveland mob crews that Phil's friends and associates later became involved in.

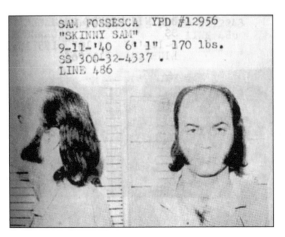

"Skinny Sam" Fossesca, close friend of Phil and another well-known alarm-bypass expert.

Joey Naples, Pittsburgh Mafia capo whom Phil helped protect until Naples went to prison. He was killed in 1991.

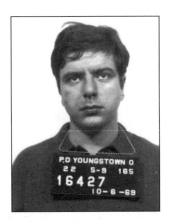

Joe DeRose, Youngstown mob hit man, was also Phil's friend and a fellow burglar. De Rose was murdered in 1981 in the Youngstown-Cleveland mob crew war.

Phil, in 1999, holding his grandson.

*Phil (seated left) with friend Tommy Marotta (seated center),
a capo in the Rochester, New York Mafia, and the rest of the "Elkton Crew"
at Elkton Federal Prison in Ohio, 2005: Sam (with cane), and standing
from left, Pete, Frank, Sal, Dave, and Adrian.*

Photo Credits: Author's collection, FBI, Cleveland Police Dept., Youngstown Police Dept.

Chapter Nineteen

B y June of 1972, the FBI was busy investigating three notorious burglaries. One was in Washington, D.C. where five burglars were arrested while breaking into a hotel called the Watergate. The others were in California and Ohio.

SPECIAL AGENT FRANK CALLEY: The bank burglary in Lordstown, Ohio, was a turning point for the United California Bank case. FBI L.A. had already requested FBI Cleveland to process Phil Christopher, the Dinsios, and others as suspects in the United California Bank burglary. But until Lordstown, the suspects' connection to the California burglary was only a theoretical one. Now a burglary with a similar MO to the California burglary—entry through the roof and the alarm being disabled—had occurred less than two months after the California burglary, and in the suspects' own backyard.

We then requested that our field offices in Chicago, Kansas City, and Cleveland check all passenger manifests on flights to L.A. in March 1972 against the Cleveland-Youngstown suspects list. That's when FBI Chicago located several of the suspects on United Airlines flights to L.A. shortly before the burglary occurred. After that we started interviewing cab drivers at LAX and showing them photos of Christopher and the Dinsios. It took some time, but we located one driver who identified one of them. He remembered several of them being in a group and that they had tipped him $100. He still had their destination on his manifest. That was a big break for us, and from there we were able trace their movements to the areas of Southgate and Lynwood, just outside L.A.

That information led us to a 1962 Oldsmobile, which was parked at a house in Tustin. It had a lot of white powder inside, like the dust from the bank vault. We suspected that the car was used in the bank burglary, and we obtained a search warrant. We located a couple of guns, some drill bits, and a rare coin.

About the same time, using phone records, we found a condominium where the burglars had stayed. It was only three miles from the bank. The condo had already been cleaned, but our evidence technicians were able to lift latent prints off some dishes and glasses in the cupboard. One of the prints was Amil Dinsio's. We knew we were close to solving what were the two biggest bank burglaries the FBI had ever seen.

PHIL: On June 2, 1972, I woke up to voices coming from downstairs. It sounded like Maggie was telling someone I wasn't home. I got out of bed and tiptoed down the hallway. When I got to the top of the steps, I looked down and saw several guys in suits.

One of them saw me and yelled, "There he is!"

There was nowhere to run, and I all I had on was short pajama bottoms. They charged up the stairs as I just stood there. When they got to the top, they grabbed my arms and said I was under arrest for probation violation. I didn't say a word. They asked me where my clothes were, and I pointed to my and Maggie's bedroom. They had me sit on the bed, then started searching around. One of them found a bag with thirty thousand dollars in it. He asked where it came from, and I told him it was from the sale of my bar, which was true.

Then they let me get dressed and handcuffed me. They walked me downstairs and out the front door. There were uniformed police outside and detective cars everywhere.

As I sat in jail, I heard that a little boy playing across the street from Amil's house had found eighty thousand dollars buried in a milk can. The FBI traced some of it to the Lordstown bank. That same day Amil and I were indicted by a Los Angeles County Grand Jury for the United California Bank score.

I was being housed in the Mahoning County Jail in Youngstown, but it wasn't all that bad. Ronnie Carrabbia was close with the captain of the jail, so I had the run of the place and was treated like a king. I had bottles of wine and J&B Scotch that I kept in the captain's office. When he left for the night, he gave me his key. I was allowed food from the outside and was even given a silk pillowcase because I was losing my hair.

My stay in Mahoning County was like a big party. Maggie was in and out all the time and even spent a few nights with me. I had a lot of visitors, and we would hang out in the captain's office and bullshit. One day I had twelve guys visiting me at the same time. This all cost me a lot in payoffs.

Charlie came to see me and was very worried about what was going on. He was very uncomfortable about being on his own. Sure enough, Charlie didn't last long. He and a couple of half-ass burglars broke into a bowling alley. They didn't jump out the alarm right, and all of them got arrested. Charlie was convicted and sentenced to twenty years because of his past history. But he couldn't face going to prison, so he turned on me. He was very cunning, and I should have seen it coming. Charlie was a reckless pill-popper who had no goals.

First he turned in the two Cleveland police supervisors who had helped me on some burglaries, and he testified in their trial. I felt awful that those two cops went to prison because of Charlie. Then he admitted his involvement in both big bank scores and testified against Amil Dinsio in the Lordstown case. I heard that Amil put out a twenty-five thousand dollar contract on Charlie, but he got placed in the witness protection program and nobody could get to him.

For thirteen months I was dragged across the country from jail to jail. Most of the time, the U.S. marshals transported me by car. Sometimes we traveled by commercial airliner. I was always handcuffed, and the marshals carried a manila envelope that said "Extremely Dangerous - Escape Risk" in big, red letters. I was put in maximum-security lock-up and solitary confinement for six months. I had a hearing in Cleveland for probation violation, was taken to Los Angeles for the United California Bank burglary trial, then back to Cleveland for the Lordstown bank case. During that period I was housed in more than a dozen different facilities across the country.

Ronnie Carrabbia was trying to help with his connections. He knew mob guys who had access to Frank Sinatra and Joe Alioto, who was the mayor of San Francisco. I heard Sinatra wouldn't even consider helping because there was too much publicity. Mayor Alioto, who was a good friend of the Jimmy "the Weasel" Fratianno, tried calling the judge in the Laguna Niguel case to help us, but the judge got mad and hung up on him.

I was paying out a lot of money for lawyers—twenty-five thousand here, fifty thousand there. I was trying to get a fix with a certain judge, but then the feds stepped in. Amil got caught on tape saying he was going to kill a witness and an FBI agent. I had nothing to do with that, but the extra attention sure didn't help my case.

The California bank score trial lasted almost six weeks. Before it was over, FBI agents located $1.5 million in bonds that the Dinsios had hidden on a farm near their house. The FBI had been digging for two weeks. The information had come from another inmate that Amil had confided in while he was being held in Los Angeles County Jail. It was another case of someone not keeping his mouth shut when he should have.

In the end everyone was convicted in the Laguna Niguel score. Everyone except Charlie. Amil and I got hit the hardest. I was sentenced to a combined twenty years for parole violation and the Laguna Niguel burglary.

The Lordstown money found in my closet was ruled inadmissible in federal court because an FBI agent was caught in a lie about the type of bag the money was found in.

He testified that the money in my closet was in an ice cream parlor bag. But I brought in a witness, one of Maggie's neighbors, who testified to having seen an FBI agent walking around with a brown paper bag. So that case against me was thrown out. But all of the money I had made went to pay the attorneys.

Amil got twenty years for both bank break-ins. James, Billy, and Harry received lesser sentences. I was labeled "the Mission Impossible Bank Burglar" by a Los Angeles radio station and sent to the federal prison at Terre Haute, Indiana. It was the last I saw of the Dinsios and my rat friend, Charlie Broeckel, who skated with my cut of the Laguna Niguel score.

Chapter Twenty

On July of 1973, two U.S. marshals transported me by car from Cleveland to the penitentiary at Terre Haute, Indiana. As we pulled in, I saw it was an old, red brick building. My first thought was how cold, depressing, and drab it looked. A prison guard holding a rifle looked down at us from the top of a forty-or fifty-foot tower that was next to the brick building. I could see at least four other towers overlooking the property.

One of the marshals yelled up, "We got one for you."

The guard lowered a bucket attached to a rope. The marshals put their guns inside, and the guard hoisted it up. A guard came outside and escorted us in as inmates peered out their windows at me. I was apprehensive but not scared. I even had a connection there already.

I was led down some stairs into the basement, which was dimly lit and damp. At the bottom of the steps was the R&D Unit—Receiving and Discharge. Another guard was there and was just stepping on a cockroach. The marshals exchanged paperwork and signatures with the guards, then left. They wished me good luck, and I thanked them because they had treated me like a person and gave me respect.

There wasn't much conversation between me and the three guards. While they were fingerprinting me, I watched another cockroach scurrying across the ceiling. The guards took my picture, and I had to fill out a medical history form. I was given a bedroll and brought into a huge holding room with two big cages and benches around the inside.

About an hour later I was brought my first food tray. There was hot meat-loaf, mashed potatoes with gravy, green beans, salad with French dressing, bread with butter, tea with sugar, and chilled plums.

The next day I was put in a dormitory with bunk beds. There were about thirty other inmates in this area, which was called A&O—Admission and Orientation. After several administrators spoke about what was expected of us and what the institution offered, we were assigned cells.

I was housed in a two-man cell with a guy from Georgia serving fourteen years for armed robbery. It was the first cell I was in that had no bars on the door. It was solid metal with a six-inch by fourteen-inch wire-mesh safety glass window. There was also a six-inch by sixteen-inch door that was used to pass food trays through without having to open the main cell door.

After the turmoil of traveling and staying in different facilities, I enjoyed the silence of my cell. I was able to settle in and organize my thoughts without so much interruption. Every now and then, I'd peer out the window and look at the cells across from me and on the second tier. I'd see other inmates look out of their cells for a moment.

The floor, walls, and ceiling of my cell were concrete and a drab brown color. Most of the other walls in the prison were off-white. There were two lockers, a small porcelain sink with push-button hot and cold running water, and a porcelain toilet. It was dim in the cell because there was only one sixty-watt light bulb in the ceiling. On the wall next to the bed was a set of headphones with about six feet of cord and a dial that read Channel One and Channel Two. All in all it wasn't bad compared to the other cells I had been kept in. The outside window had a solid iron frame with small, thick panes of glass. There was nothing to see outside except cornfields.

I put the sheet and pillow case on my bed and lay down. It was like being in a luxury hotel compared to the short-term facilities I had been in for the past thirteen months. All that moving around was over now and I could relax. I wasn't thrilled with my sentence, but on the other hand, I accepted responsibility for what I did. A lot of guys I met in the different jails across the country would complain about their conviction and sentence. They would blame the police, prosecutor, jury, or judge. I realized that doing time was just one of the risks that went along with being a burglar. It was just part of the game.

Right after I got into the compound, a prisoner walked up and introduced himself as Chuck Bartolli. Chuck and I had a mutual friend, a burglar from Chicago, who had told him I was being sent to Terre Haute. Chuck was connected to the organized crime outfit in Chicago. He introduced me to so many guys in one day that my head was spinning. Most of them were Italian and connected to the mobs in Chicago and New York and St. Louis. They were all friendly and asked me what I needed. They sent me a big care package of food, toiletries, and clothing. At Terre Haute we wore khaki military-style pants and shirts from 6:00 a.m. until 3:30 p.m., Monday through Friday. But at all other times we were allowed to wear street clothes, like sweatpants and sweatshirts, or shorts and T-shirts and tennis shoes.

Chuck and his friends gave me a grand tour of the joint, which was their way of welcoming a new inmate. The main corridor at Terre Haute was long, about a quarter mile. In the middle was the control room, with windows allowing the guards to see up and down the corridor. The windows were protected with bars.

Across from the control room was the chow hall, and above that was the gym. On each side of the control room were eight or ten units, which were basically cell blocks and dormitories. There were two tiers to each unit. The cells were all single-man with solid doors. There were also a few dormitories. When you would walk into each unit it was dim because the lights were on the thirty-foot-high ceiling and were spaced far apart. Then there was the second tier of cells, which had very narrow walkway designed for just one person to be on. The doors on those cells slid on a track because of the narrow walkway.

There was a room off the control area, where only one particular inmate was permitted. During the night and on weekends, he operated two record players that used the big 33-1/3 rpm albums and 45 rpm singles. The music was piped into the cells and could be listened to through headphones.

Inmates who violated rules were sent to G-Block at the east end of the corridor. It was better known as the hole and consisted of twenty cells with bars.

There was a lot to do at Terre Haute. The recreation yard was divided into the main yard and east yard, which were separated by a gate. The main yard had two softball diamonds, a bocce ball court, an eighteen-hole putt-putt course, a quarter-mile track, a workout area with weights and chin-up bars, a shuffle-board court, badminton, horseshoes, and a volleyball court. There were two stainless steel toilets and a four-foot-long urinal surrounded by a brick wall that was four feet high. And there were concrete bleachers about eighty feet wide and thirty feet high for the inmates to watch the baseball games. The east yard also had a softball diamond, six handball courts, and four tennis courts. The whole recreation area was in view of the guard towers.

On weekends the prison recreation department would show movies in the big gym. It was comfortable in the spring and fall, but in the summer you would sweat to death from the heat. And in the winter you had to wear a coat and stocking cap to stay warm. We would sit in folding metal chairs. It was very dark when the movie was on, so everybody would bunch together in their cliques for protection.

The food in the institution wasn't like home, but you sure had enough of it, except for meat, which was rationed. But every time there was a fight and somebody was killed, we were served steak. The best way to quiet a prison down is to feed the inmates a good meal.

At night the cockroaches and mice came out in force. The mice would scurry back and forth along the floor, picking up little bits of food. Sometimes you could look out the windows at night and see pigeons flying in circles. The next morning you could go out in the rec yard and see pigeon feathers where a hawk had snatched one out of the air. In summertime there were many flies because of the farm camp. The flies were so brutal that the area had to be defogged.

There was always an air of tension at Terre Haute. It was one of the most violent prisons and was known as the gladiator school of the federal system. In my first year, seven inmates were murdered. A lot of the prisoners who were killed were caught off guard at 6:00 a.m. when the cell doors were unlocked. Most guys wedged their doors closed while they slept so that nobody could run in on them.

I ran with a mostly Italian gang, and none of the other prisoners gave us any problems. But even if you stayed out of trouble yourself, you had to be constantly alert to avoid getting caught in the middle of someone else's fight.

One weekend morning two black religious groups clashed just as I entered the east yard. The guard locked the gate just in time and confined the fight to the main yard. About fifty prisoners were swinging bats, golf clubs, pipes, two-by-fours, and horseshoes. When a guard in the tower fired a few shots in the air, the fight stopped. There was blood all over, and even teeth. The next morning two buses pulled up to Receiving and Discharge to ship the prisoners to different institutions.

At night big spotlights would shine around the grounds. The area was surrounded by a double row of fences, which were about fifteen feet high, twelve feet apart, and topped with razor wire. An alarm wire ran along the top and would alert the towers if someone tried to escape by cutting the wire.

As the months went by, I saw almost every inch of Terre Haute except the business office, which was up front. The warden had his office there. No inmates were allowed in the business offices except the farm camp prisoners who cleaned them. The farm camp was considered a cushy place to do time. It supplied meat, milk, corn, and potatoes for the entire institution. There was a tunnel that ran from the prison out to the power house where the farm camp prisoners worked. Hot water from the powerhouse boilers traveled through pipes in the tunnel and into the prison for heat. In the winter the steam heat kept most of the prison very warm.

The guards in Terre Haute were all big farm boys. When a group of them ran down the main corridor during an emergency, the whole building vibrated. They were definitely hard-nosed but fair. There were some jerks for guards, but that went for convicts, too. The guards in the towers were armed with rifles, but the regular guards didn't carry guns. Sometimes the guards would administer their own discipline to some hard-case inmate in the tunnel. Then he'd be transferred somewhere else to lick his wounds.

It took about eight hours to drive from Cleveland to Terre Haute, so I only got visits once every few months. When we had visitors, we were strip-searched before and immediately after the visit. You had to stand naked in front of the guards, shake your hair out, and show behind your ears. Then you had to let them inspect the inside of your mouth, show both sides of your hands, then raise your arms to show your armpits. Next you lifted up your privates so they could see down there, and lifted one foot up at a time to show the bottoms. Finally you had to turn around, bend over, and cough. What a nice way to start and end visits.

The guards were looking for drugs coming in or money going out from inmates selling the drugs. Some prisoners would have the drugs hidden in balloons, which they would actually swallow during a visit. Later they would stick their fingers down their throat to vomit up the drugs. If that didn't work, they would take a laxative. Then they'd put on rubber gloves and rummage through their shit. It was gross, but they did it. Marijuana, cocaine, and heroin came in through the visiting room. Once in a while, an inmate would bribe a guard to bring in contraband. Usually someone would find out, the guard would be fired, and the inmate sent to the hole.

There was no limit on the number of visitors you could have. My mother, father, and Maggie came to see me several times. Sometimes during the summer months, aunts and uncles would come with my parents. But my favorite visitor was my grandmother— my father's mother—and my parents brought her every time.

My grandmother was a typical, heavy-set Italian lady and was in her eighties. The first time she saw me in prison she said, "You thinka you a bigga shot? Now you a bigga shit."

My grandmother would hide dried sausages inside her dress, hanging them around her neck with string. My mother would sneak in homemade cookies, and my father might bring a nice chunk of provolone. I would eat this food during our visit before I got searched again.

It was always great to have visitors, but when it was over I was sad to see them go, and I was always mentally exhausted when I got back to my cell. I'd be lying there staring up at the ceiling and feeling like I'd run ten miles and lifted weights in the same day.

Chapter Twenty-One

The time in Terre Haute went by pretty fast. I tried to keep myself busy and forget about the street because if you think about the street too much, it will make you do hard time. I worked out with weights and ran a lot to stay in shape. Maggie and I wrote a lot of letters back and forth, and I called her when I could. I asked her to marry me, but she wanted to wait until I got released.

My prison jobs also kept me busy. My first job was as an assistant in the prison hospital. An inmate named Greg, who was from Cleveland and was a physician's assistant, got me a job working with him. I worked during the days from 7:30 a.m. to 3:30 p.m. I also worked with an outside lab technician and learned how to draw blood from the inmates. I got good at hitting the vein on the first try.

There was an old doctor who would come in from his outside practice to take care of the inmates. He looked like Rip Van Winkle, and his hands shook when he examined patients. The doctor only came in once a week, but a physician's assistant was available twenty-four hours a day.

The hospital had three floors. The bottom floor had the outpatient department, exam rooms, administrative offices, and the x-ray room. The second floor had a therapy room and a few holding cells for quarantined patients. There was a small operating room on the third floor, where the doctor performed minor operations. And there were two open wards with hospital beds for very sick inmates.

That's when I got close-up experience with prison violence. It often occurred over very minor things, like the two black guys who got into an argument over a television program. The smaller guy got a metal peg used to play horseshoes, snuck up behind the other guy, and hit him in the back of the head. I was on duty in the hospital that day, and Greg and I grabbed a gurney and ran down to the unit. We found the guy lying face down and unconscious on some stairs. Blood was running down each step, and the guy's head was soaked dark red.

Greg and I picked him up and got him on the gurney. There was so much blood that my hands were slipping, and I almost dropped him. We started running down the main corridor to the hospital. I was doing okay until I saw that his head wasn't completely on the gurney. I lifted it gently with my hand and shuddered. The whole back of his head felt like a wet sponge. I helped Greg put an airway tube down his throat and an IV in his arm, but he died on the way to the outside hospital. The prisoner who killed him got ten years on top of the thirty he was already doing.

Most of the killings were done with shanks. Some of the homemade blades were so long that they looked like swords. One time a guy's head was practically severed. There was one fight in which an inmate taped the shank to his hand. There was another murder in which an inmate was stabbed so many times, they had trouble counting.

There were suicides, too. I remember one where a guy tried to kill himself after receiving a Dear John letter from his wife. But he cut both arms straight up and down instead of across the wrists. He lived but had to get almost one hundred fifty sutures on each arm.

After working in the hospital for about a year, I got a job as a clerk in the assistant warden's office. It was a good job. The AW was Mr. Lippman, a retired police detective from Detroit. He was a big man, about six feet two inches and solid, and he had a bald head. He reminded me of Telly Savalas. Mr. Lippman never said much to the inmates.

Basically I kept track of all the housing records—which inmates were assigned to which units and cells. I was responsible for the request forms inmates would fill out if they wanted to move to a different unit because of a new job or to be closer to a friend. If you had been incarcerated for a long time with no disciplinary problems, you could move into the honor unit to live in a one-man cell and get away from the idiots. I also filed the requests for inmates who wanted to go to the hospital, dental lab, or an educational program.

From working in the AW's office, I got to meet a lot of important prison officials. I made it a point to be friendly with them. I especially tried to make a good impression for the parole examiners, whose hearing room was right across from where I worked. I would score a few brownie points by getting them pastry and coffee. One of them, a black guy from Cleveland, used to be a parole officer for the State of Ohio. He took a liking to me and used to call me "Homey."

I had been at Terre Haute about two-and-a-half years when I first went before the parole board. I could have seen them earlier, but I had learned it was better to get some time under your belt and give them a good report on your progress.

I was allowed to have someone represent me at the parole board, and I chose my boss, Mr. Lasker. He was the secretary for the AW and the type of person who never did anything wrong. He didn't say too much, but I thought he did a good job representing me. The parole board told me to come back in one year, which was good because they could have said five years.

A guy named Mr. Johnson was always coming in to see the AW, and after a while I started talking to him and learned that he was in charge of the farm camp. Eventually I asked him if he needed any clerks on the farm camp, but he said no. I told him to please keep me in mind if he ever needed one. The seed was planted, and now it was a matter of time.

There was a lot of gambling, drugs, and homemade hooch in the joint but

I kept busy and stayed away from it. I did try some raisin jack once, but it made me sick, and I said that was the last time. The homosexuals tried a couple of times to get me to go in their cells, but I told them I loved women, not men.

Keeping busy and staying out of trouble paid off. In the summer of 1975, Mr. Johnson came into the AW's office and asked me if I still wanted a clerk's job on the farm camp. I said of course I did. He looked at my boss, Mr. Lasker, who said it would be up to the AW, Mr. Lippman. Mr. Johnson told me he would talk to the AW for me. I was excited because I knew this would be an important step for me and would look very good at my next parole hearing.

Mr. Johnson was in the AW's office for a few minutes when he opened the door and told me to come in. I went in and stood in front of Mr. Lippman's desk.

"So, Christopher, you want to leave me and go to the camp as a clerk?" he said.

"Yes. I hear it is a lot nicer and has a lot more fresh air."

"Well, you've done a good job for me. That's all for now."

I left Mr. Lippman's office and waited. A few minutes later, Mr. Johnson came out of the office and looked at Mr. Lasker.

"You'd better find yourself a new clerk," he told him. "I'm taking Christopher to the farm camp with me."

I thanked Mr. Johnson, and he left the office. I was so excited I had a hard time typing. I couldn't wait to write home and tell my mother and father. Word spread quickly through the institution, and all my friends were congratulating me.

A few weeks later, I was putting all of my property into a big duffel bag and a couple of smaller bags. Everyone I knew was coming to my cell, shaking hands with me and saying goodbye. And of course, the older Italians were giving me a hug and kiss on the cheek. I knew it was out of friendship and I respected them, but I hated being hugged and kissed like that. I just preferred a firm handshake and look in the eye.

I carried my duffel bag to the rear gate. After I went through the first gate, it closed.

"So you're going to be a farmer now, huh, Christopher?" the guard said, while looking at his paperwork.

"Yeah. It should be different."

"It sure is different."

He motioned to the guard in the tower. I looked back, and some of my close friends were watching me from the rec yard. The second gate went up. I walked through, and it closed behind me. I turned around and waved to the guys. They were smiling, waving back, and giving me the thumbs up.

A small yellow bus pulled up, and Tony LaBarbera was driving it. Tony had been the front man for a big Chicago trucking company owned by the mob. I'd heard he was a pretty tough character in his day. I just looked around as we drove up the road to the farm camp dormitory, feeling like a ball and chain had been cut from my ankle. We passed the dairy and slaughterhouse, then we came to the dorm.

Tony wheeled the bus up to the front of the dorm and parked. He helped me with my bags, and we walked to the front entrance where there was a guard.

"So you made the farm camp, huh, Christopher?"

"Yeah," I said, smiling.

The guard told me which dorm room and bunk I was assigned to. Tony showed me the way and gave me a little tour. There were single-man rooms and dorms for six, eight, and twelve guys. I was assigned to an eight-man dorm but eventually got my own cell. There were no bars on the doors and windows, and you could walk around as you pleased as long as you were in your room for count. Some inmates would even have their girlfriends come to the edge of the farm, then sneak out and meet them for sex.

There were two big TV rooms with soft, comfortable chairs. Everything seemed so spacious and clean, and the air nice and sweet from the cornfields.

I said to Tony, "This is great."

"Yeah, it sure is a relaxing atmosphere out here compared to the inside."

As the days went by, I became more familiar with the running of the farm camp, which supplied all the beef, pork, and milk for the Terre Haute prison and for the Marion Penitentiary in Illinois, which replaced Alcatraz when it was shut down. I went over to the dairy and saw how the inmate workers milked the cows and pasteurized the milk. I saw where they raised the pigs. It was funny because the pigs were all lying on each other.

I also checked out the slaughterhouse and saw the inmate workers killing pigs. One would hit the pig in the head with a sledgehammer, and another would cut its throat. While I was there, one pig's throat didn't get cut completely, and it got up and ran. The pig was squealing as an inmate chased him, swinging wildly with the sledgehammer. The pig was coming right for me, and I started heading for the door. The inmate finally stopped the pig in its tracks. After watching how they skinned and gutted these animals, I thought I'd never eat meat again.

Farm camp inmates had jobs in the kitchen, the power house, garage, and guard training center. Another group operated the farm equipment used to cut the corn fields and turn the ground up. Most of the corn was used to feed the livestock. There was a Safety and Sanitation Department, which was all Italian inmates. They had a fire engine and a green pick-up truck that everyone called the "dago-mobile." Other farm camp prisoners cut the grass around the property and cleaned the business offices at the main institution. Tony LaBarbera's job was to transport the inmates back and forth to their jobs.

As a clerk I had the same basic duties as when I was in the main institution, but on a smaller scale since there were only a couple hundred inmates on the farm camp. I also did some running around for the two case managers assigned to the camp.

As the months went by, guys I was close with on the inside started making it out to the farm camp. Most of them were from Chicago or St. Louis, like Willie Orlando. He was doing time for loan sharking. There was also Pete Cascarelli from Youngstown, who was in for a short stretch. And I was friends with Tony Colangelo, who was with the Colombo crime family in New York. I was much younger, but they all had taken a liking to me. We started to have a good crew on the farm camp and even had our own Italian-American Club.

While on the farm camp, I was able to make more phone calls to my parents and Maggie. When I first went to prison, we were only allowed one ten-minute phone call every three months. Your counselor would dial the number and sit across from you, timing the conversation. But around the time I was transferred to the farm camp, more phone lines were put in. In the main institution, inmates had to schedule use of the phone, but on the farm camp, we would could call any time, even without going to our counselors, as long as we had money in our account to cover the charges.

Visiting was less restrictive on the camp as well. On weekends visitors could purchase a meal ticket for $1.25 from the guard at the front desk, then they would stand in line with us to eat. The inmates with visitors got to go ahead of the other prisoners. And farm camp prisoners didn't get searched for their visits. Of course, when our visitors would come, they would drop off a package at a certain spot where it would be retrieved by whatever inmate was working the cornfields. We had some good meals with the food that was brought in this way. Sometimes we would sneak down to the Wabash River, which was only a hundred yards away, to go fishing. We would bring our catch back and cook it in the kitchen.

One day I went to the kitchen to see what Willie Orlando was cooking. He was usually making some kind of dessert. Frank Tocco was in there with Willie, and they were busy preparing dinner.

"What smells so good?" I said.

Frank said, "It's rabbit.'

"Rabbit? You gotta be kidding."

Willie opened the oven door, and I looked in at whatever was cooking in there. It had little ribs, but I couldn't tell what it was. It could have been a cat for all I knew.

"Where did you guys get a rabbit from?"

"The dayshift guard ran into it on his way to work," Frank answered.

Road kill, I thought to myself.

"Christ, that's sick," I said, shaking my head as Frank and Willie laughed.

I stayed in the kitchen, and after a while, they took the rabbit out of the oven and sat down at a table in the kitchen. I sat down with them, and they asked me to try some.

"No thanks."

"C'mon, Phil. Try some. You'll like it," Frank assured me.

Frank and Willie sure looked like they were enjoying this rabbit. After a few minutes, my curiosity got the best of me and I tried some.

"Hey, this is great," I said.

Frank and Willie were laughing.

Food was a big thing on the farm camp. As long as things were peaceful, the warden and guards didn't care if we got some food in from the outside.

Once a year, our Italian-American Club was allowed to have a banquet, and we were allowed to have one person each from the street eat with us. We'd also invite the warden, assistant wardens, and captains. We learned from Frank DeLeggo, an older guy from Chicago, how to make cheese from milk. It took a lot of milk to make a little bit of cheese, but that was no problem since we had the dairy right here.

Now that we knew how to make cheese, we decided to make lasagna for our banquet. We began stealing milk from the dairy, bringing it to the kitchen, and pouring it into fifty gallon vats used to make soup. The cheese product would curdle to the top, and we'd skim it off with a strainer, put it in a cloth bag, then hang it up to drain. It seemed like we went through two hundred gallons of milk to make just enough cheese for our lasagna. Well, the lasagna came out just great. The warden and staff members couldn't get over how good it was. They didn't know about lasagna because they were meat-and-potatoes men.

Since there wasn't as much to do on the farm camp, time seemed to go slower than in the main institution. But my parole hearing was approaching, and being on the farm camp would be a plus for me.

Chapter Twenty-Two

On the day of my hearing, I was very nervous. I had asked my case manager to come with me and say some positive things. We went into the hearing room, and the two parole examiners introduced themselves and told us to sit down. There was a tape recorder on the table between us. One of the examiners was the black guy from Cleveland, but the other one did all the talking. He asked if we had anything to say. My case manager told them that I was a good worker and he felt I was ready for the street.

Then the examiner asked me if I had anything to add. My hands were perspiring. I told them I was ready to return to society and be a good, law-abiding citizen. I knew that's what they wanted to hear. They asked if I had employment lined up, and I told them I didn't know what I was going to do but I had a lot of job offers. The parole examiner was going through my file and commenting on how many positive letters were sent on my behalf about employment opportunities. He saw that I hadn't been in any trouble at Terre Haute and was impressed with my progress. After a few more good comments, he asked me to step out of the room. My case manager stayed in a couple more minutes, then he came out. He told me the parole examiners would call me back in when they made their decision.

I was pacing back and forth. My hands were still perspiring, and now my heart was racing. Ten long minutes went by, then I heard them yell my name. I opened the door and went in by myself this time. I sat down, and the same examiner who did the talking before told me they both agreed to give me parole. He said they were undecided whether to parole me in four months or six months, but they'd send their recommendation to the main office in Kansas City. I was so happy when I got up and thanked them both, then walked out with a big smile.

My case manager and some other inmates asked me how it went. I told them and they congratulated me. Then I headed down the hall to the telephone. As I passed my friends, I told them I made parole and they were happy for me. Then I got on the phone to call my parents. My mother answered the phone, and I got all choked up when I heard her voice. But I kept my composure because a bunch of guys were watching me.

My mother was very happy and yelled to my father, "Joe, they recommended Philip for parole in four or six months."

"That's great," I could hear my father answer back.

I asked my mother to let Maggie know. After we hung up, I had to wipe my eyes a little. Then I went back to my cell, lay down on my bunk, and started daydreaming about the streets.

It was a month later when my case manager informed me that my parole papers were in. In three months I would be sent to a halfway house in Cleveland called Harbor Light Mission. After a month or so there, I'd be officially paroled.

A high school friend of mine named Matt was a boss at the Board of Elections in Cleveland and said he could get me a job with the Republican Party. I thought politics would be a good field for me because there was a place you had a license to steal. Matt said I could start as soon as I got out of the halfway house. Then when I got my driver's license, I would be Robert Hughes's right hand man. Hughes was the chairman for the Republican Party.

I never paid much attention to politics until this opportunity came along.

Then I started noticing Hughes's name a lot in the newspaper. I learned he was a very powerful figure and did a lot of traveling, especially to Detroit. Matt said he met with a lot of people, including big politicians, union officials, and mob-connected guys, and needed someone he could trust to back him up and keep his mouth shut. I felt I could do a good job because I knew how to carry myself and make people feel important. Most people like to feel that way. Personally I never cared about being important. Just show me the money.

On Christmas Day several of us were cleaning up after the holiday party the warden and guards had had with their families at the training center. While we were there, we had some food from the street. We had baby squid and were cooking linguini with tomato sauce while we were cleaning. It was going to be a little Christmas dinner and celebration for my upcoming parole. The sauce smelled so good.

Suddenly one of the guys yelled, "Here comes the warden, captain, and superintendent."

We started hiding everything quickly before they got in. They walked in, looked around, and asked how we were doing. The warden commented on how well we cleaned up after the mess they made. Then they turned around and were leaving. I thought to myself, hurry up and get out so we can eat. When they reached the door, suddenly the warden turned around.

"Have a nice day, and you boys enjoy your macaroni sauce because it sure smells good," he said.

The captain and superintendent were smiling at us as they left. We laughed about the ordeal as we brought our food out and started eating. That was the best meal I'd had in years.

With only a few days to go before I was paroled, it seemed like time stopped. I kept thinking about the streets and my family. It was going to be a new year and a new start for my life. I was running, lifting weights, and playing handball often so that I could be tired at night, but I was still having trouble sleeping.

The day before I was supposed to leave, I gave away all my things, like my weightlifting belt and gloves, to my friends. All I needed was a pair of shoes, pants, and a shirt to leave. Needless to say, I didn't sleep at all that night. I stayed up all night drinking coffee with the guys I lived with. They were happy for me. We talked about everything under the sun, but the only thing I recall was looking at the clock often and watching out the window at the bats snatching bugs out of the air by the big spotlight.

It was December 29, 1976, and daylight finally arrived. I had two hours to go before I'd be heading home. I went to breakfast with a bunch of my friends, but I wasn't hungry. Afterward I met with my case manager, who gave me some paperwork for the halfway house. After that I was just pacing the main hallway and looking out at the road for my mother and father, who were supposed to pick me up. My closest friends were with me and seemed to be as excited as I was. They were even watching out the window for my parents.

Suddenly Willie Orlando yelled, "Hey, Phil, here they come."

My heart started beating hard, and I got all choked up. I went to the main door and in walked my mother, father, and Maggie, which was a nice surprise. I could feel tears starting to come. It took a lot not to cry in front of the other guys as I hugged and kissed Maggie and my parents. Then I turned around to see about forty guys standing behind me—inmates, guards, case managers, counselors, and Mr. Johnson, the superintendent. I shook hands with everyone as they wished me well. The older Italians hugged me and gave me a kiss on the cheek.

Then one of the guards said loudly, "Okay, let Phil go home, and you guys get back to your jobs."

There were lots of laughs and a few boos. I laughed as I walked out the door and down to my father's car. It felt like a ton of bricks off my back. I got in the backseat and leaned up to kiss my mother and father. My mother said she brought one of my old winter jackets, but I didn't need it because the car was already very warm.

On the way home, I was very quiet and just looked at the cars and people we passed. After a while I was relaxed and started talking. My father told me a bunch of the family wanted to see me. I told him I'd rather not see anyone right away. I just wanted to be alone for a while and clear up my thoughts.

It was a seven-hour ride but went fast. As we got close to Cleveland, the area started to look familiar. First we pulled up to the Harbor Light Mission downtown, where I was to report. We rang the button, and a man's voice came over the intercom. I told him who I was, and he buzzed us in and met us by the door. He introduced himself as a counselor and took my paperwork from Terre Haute. He said I could have the weekend off, but I had to report back Sunday night by 10:00 p.m. I thought to myself, this is great.

We got back in the car and headed toward my parents' house. When we got into Collinwood, the neighborhood looked different. The trees seemed to envelope the roadway and sidewalks more. And it seemed the yards were more manicured.

We got to my parents' house, and my brother and his wife and kids were there. We all sat down at the dining room table, and a few minutes later my grandmother came walking in. I got up and gave her a big hug and kiss. My mother and grandmother were bringing all kinds of food to the table and trying to get me to eat, but I hardly ate anything.

Then, one by one, my aunts, uncles, and cousins started arriving. Pretty soon, cars were parked up and down the street on both sides. And you could barely move in the house. There was a lot of noise with all the people talking, the phone ringing non-stop, and kids running up and down the stairs. The cigarette smoke from some of the older kids down in the basement was drifting up and getting to be too much for me. It was nice to see everyone, but I was still a little unsettled.

I had a glass of my father's homemade wine and started to unwind a little. Then I tried to talk to Maggie, but she was standoffish. She was still sweet to me, but I could tell things had changed between us. I didn't care, though. It was just great to be home.

After a couple of hours, everyone started leaving one by one. When they were all gone, the house looked like a tornado had come through. I tried to help my mother and Maggie clean up, but they made me sit down.

"Ma, I'm not an invalid. I can help clean up," I said.

"No, no, Philip. You just sit down and relax. Maggie and I will take care of it."

After Maggie helped my mother, she said she was going home. I kissed her goodbye and told her I'd see her tomorrow.

It felt so good to be home. My father was lying on the couch, and I was sitting in a comfortable chair watching TV. But my mind was wandering. I was thinking that just twenty-four hours ago, I was on the farm camp at Terre Haute, and now I was free.

It had been a long day, but I still wasn't tired. My mother came into the living room and asked if I was cold. I told her it was a little cool. Before I knew it, she was neatly draping a blanket over me.

I said, "Ma, I'm not helpless. I can cover myself." I felt like I was being treated like a child.

My mother sat down on the chair next to me, and we chatted for a while. My father fell asleep on the couch, and I finally decided to go up to bed. It had been years since I slept upstairs in my parents' house. I got into one of the little single beds that my brother and I had slept in as kids. It sure made a lot of noise as I moved around to get comfortable.

After breakfast the next morning, I decided to go for a walk in the neighborhood. I walked slowly, noticing new cars and faces in the neighborhood. The roar of a train going by was a familiar sound.

I walked over to Maggie's house, which was just on the next block. I knew her kids would all be at school, and I was hoping to get lucky. We talked for a little while, but I couldn't get to first base. She said I needed to give her a little time. I wasn't upset because I knew I'd get it sooner or later. From her or another woman.

Sunday afternoon came quickly. Maggie drove me to the halfway house and dropped me off. I got there a few hours early because I wanted to see what the place was like. The receptionist buzzed me in and told me my room number. On the third floor, I opened the door to a small, dingy room with an old single bed. The shade on the window looked like it was ready to fall apart. I lay down on the bed, which felt like a board, and tried to make the best of it.

The next morning I met the commander of the halfway house, who told me all the rules and showed me a little coffee shop on the first floor where I could get breakfast. On weekdays I would be allowed to leave the halfway house as early as 6:00 a.m. but had to be back by 10:00 p.m. I would have the weekends off but had to be back by 10:00 p.m. on Sundays. On Saturdays I would have to call to confirm that I was spending the night at my parents' house.

After getting the lowdown on the halfway house, my friend Matt picked me up and took me to Robert Hughes's office. Matt mentioned again that Hughes was a powerful figure in the Republican Party who was close with the presidents when the Republicans were in power. I asked him if he thought Hughes knew someone who could get me off parole. Matt said he was sure Mr. Hughes knew someone who could help. That sounded good to me.

We got to Hughes's office, and Matt introduced me. He was tall with salt and pepper hair and about fifty years old.

"Nice to meet you, Mr. Hughes," I said.

"Call me Bob. I've heard a lot of good things about you, Phil. Glad to have you on the team. Do you have your driver's license?"

"Not yet. I've got to take the test first."

"Well, as soon as you get it, we'll put you to work."

"In the meantime," he said, turning to Matt, "take care of him with whatever he needs."

This was working out just as I thought it would.

Matt then took me over to the Board of Elections, where I was to work in the voting machines department.

The days started going pretty well, and I was feeling more relaxed than when I first came home. But then a couple of times when I got to the halfway house, the receptionist told me that some woman newspaper reporter from the Plain Dealer had called several times and wanted to talk to me. I couldn't figure out why someone from the newspaper would want to talk to me. About a week later, I walked in and the receptionist said the reporter was on the phone for me. He asked me to please talk to her so she'd stop calling. I took the phone from him and said hello.

"Is this Philip Christopher?" she asked.

"Yes it is."

"Mr. Christopher, my name is Mary Jane Woge. I'm a reporter with the Plain Dealer. I'd like to ask you some questions."

I didn't say anything.

"It seems like you've done very well," she said. "You were sentenced to twenty years in prison and only served four."

I just listened.

"Can you explain how you got out of prison so quickly?"

I said, "I'd rather not discuss anything."

"How about telling me how you feel about Charlie Broeckel."

"That's all done and over," I said. "I'd rather just let it go."

Then she got to the real reason she called.

"I'm writing a book and would like to sit down and ask you some questions."

"I'm getting on with my life and I'd rather not discuss anything."

She was getting annoyed and being more persistent. I was being nice, but she just didn't want to take no for an answer.

"It wouldn't take long, perhaps and hour or so. It's going to be about the United California Bank case. I could come out to Harbor Light tomorrow."

"No, ma'am. I'd rather not talk about it."

"Well, you're going to be in the book whether you like it or not," she said.

"Whatever," I said.

She slammed the phone down, and I handed the receiver to the desk man and told him he probably wouldn't be hearing from her again. He thanked me and added that she was becoming a real pain. I went up to my room and went to sleep.

The next morning I woke and went down to the little restaurant, ordered coffee, and bought a Cleveland Plain Dealer to read while waiting for my father to pick me up. As soon as I opened the newspaper, my eyes found the front page headline. I'll never forget the date—January 16.

It read, Superthief Out on Parole. Loot Still Missing.

I knew immediately it was about me, and my heart started beating hard. As I read through the story, I had a bad feeling that it was going to cause me problems.

Chapter Twenty-Three

A few minutes later, I saw my father pull up. When I got in the car, he didn't say anything about the article, so I figured he hadn't seen it. I decided not to mention it until we got home because I knew he'd get upset and start yelling. But as soon as we got inside my parents' house, my mother was standing at the top of the stairs with a newspaper in her hand. I shook my head, knowing it was going to be a bad day.

"Joe, did you see the newspaper?" she said to my father, while coming down the steps.

He said no.

"This son-of-a-bitch newspaper lady is complaining because Philip was only in jail four years."

She gave the paper to my father, and he started reading.

"Did you see it?" my mother asked me as my father started yelling and swearing.

"Yeah, ma, I saw it."

"How come you didn't tell me?" my father said.

"Because I knew you'd get upset and start yelling."

Now my head was hurting, so I went into the living room and lay down on the couch. My father was finishing the article and calling the reporter a dirty, rotten, son-of-a-bitch. I knew my mother and father were only upset because they loved me.

They finally calmed down, only to get riled up again when the phone rang, which it never did this early. It was the first of many calls my parents got from my aunts, uncles, and cousins about the newspaper story

About an hour later, Matt picked me up. He'd already read the article and asked me if I wanted the day off, but I said I'd rather work to get my mind off it. We drove to the Board of Elections but only put in half a day. Afterward I had Matt drop me off at Maggie's house, but first I picked up a box of pastries for her. When I got there, her eyes were bloodshot and puffy.

"What's wrong," I said.

"Don't they ever stop?"

"What do you mean?"

"Why did they have to blast you in the newspaper?"

"Don't pay attention to it."

I got her calmed down, and we went up to her bedroom and made love. Afterward we went down to the kitchen, she made a pot of coffee, and we ate some of the pastries I brought.

We were just chatting about things in general—her kids, my plans for the future, and the possibility of us getting married—when suddenly I heard a car pull in the driveway. I couldn't see who it was and figured it was one of her make-up customers. Then there was a knock at the side door behind me. I turned around and saw two guys in suits. Right away my heart started pounding. Maggie went to the door and asked who it was. They showed her identification and said they were U.S. marshals and wanted to talk to me. I went to the door and told them to come in.

One of them said, "Phil, can we talk to you in the car?"

"Okay," I said, figuring it was about the newspaper article.

Maggie had a pained looked on her face.

"You're not taking him away, are you?" she asked.

"Ma'am, we want to talk to Phil."

I could see she was getting nervous.

"I'll be right back," I said as she leaned over and kissed me.

I got in the back of the car, and the marshals sat in front. Then they showed me an order from the parole commission in Kansas City to rescind my parole and detain me for another hearing. I gritted my teeth, took a deep breath, and shook my head. I'd thought the bad times were behind me. I looked up at the house and Maggie was watching from inside. She was crying.

The marshals told me a newspaper reporter caused all this. I asked if I could go tell Maggie or at least yell to her, but they said no. There was nothing I could do. I thought about running, but there was no handle on the inside of the door. And the marshals were just doing their job. They asked me to put my hands up so that they could handcuff me, and I did. As we backed out of the driveway I wanted to wave at Maggie but she wasn't looking out the window anymore.

When we got to the street, the marshals turned east instead of west to go downtown. They said they were taking me to Lake County Jail, about forty-five minutes outside of Cleveland, to keep me away from the newspaper and television reporters waiting for me at the county jail. They said there were bunch of them with TV cameras set up.

I asked the marshals if they knew what was going to happen next, but they had no idea. I was sick to my stomach. I could always accept being arrested for a crime, but in this case I did my time and didn't do anything to violate my parole.

When we got to the jail, the corrections officer had a form to fill out and asked the marshals if they had any paperwork on me. The marshals said no and told the jailer my name was John Smith. They told him I was a special case and didn't know how long I'd be housed there. They asked him to put me in a cell where nobody would bother me.

After that was over, the marshals took me aside and removed the handcuffs. They said the reason they didn't use my name was because the newspaper reporters would be calling the jails to find me. It was nice that they didn't want me to be hassled, but I really didn't care at this point.

After the marshals left, the jailer brought me to a block with three empty cells and put me in one of them. It had a single bed with a plastic mattress and pillow with no linen, a stainless steel sink, and toilet and a fixed metal chair and desk. I just lay down, exhausted from the stressful day, staring at the ceiling until I fell asleep.

When I woke up, I couldn't tell what time it was because there were no windows around. I got up and was pacing back and forth in the little cell. Finally I heard a door open, and a guard brought breakfast in. I asked what time it was, and he said 6:00 a.m. Then I asked him how I could make a phone call. He told me I would have to wait for the dayshift to come on. I ate a little bit and waited for what seemed like hours before I heard the outside door open again. A different guard came in and said I had visitors. I asked who it was, and he said it was my family. I felt some life come back to me because I had been so down and depressed the last day.

I got pretty choked up when I saw my mother and father. I loved them very much, and I often think of the pain I must have put them through. I wonder where my head was, but when it came to wanting money, I was like a junkie.

I was so glad to see them, my brother, and Maggie, even though they were on the other side of the thick glass, and we had to talk on an intercom phone. They told me they had a lawyer coming to represent me. Maggie and my parents were telling me not worry and that everything would turn out okay, but I didn't believe it. I had a bad feeling in my stomach.

The next day the attorney came to see me and said we had a hearing in two days. I asked him how it looked, and he said they really didn't have a reason to take my parole away. I understood what he meant, but I wasn't on parole yet. Once I got out of the halfway house, I'd be on parole. I was still under the jurisdiction of the Bureau of Prisons. There wasn't anything else to discuss, so the attorney left.

The days were going by slowly. I was getting unusually tired and just lying down in my cell a lot. I figured the stress was really getting to me. This Mary Jane Woge must have had really had it in for me because I was reading her articles about me in the newspapers every day.

On the day of my hearing, the marshals drove me to the federal courthouse in Cleveland. They headed around to a side door instead of the back tunnel entrance they usually use for prisoners. I didn't have to ask why. I looked at the back entrance, and there was nothing but reporters and TV cameras.

The marshals escorted me into the courtroom, and I saw my family sitting in the back. The hearing was a waste of time. Before I knew it, I was in a federal car with two U.S. marshals on the road back to Terre Haute federal prison. I had been free nineteen days. I didn't even get a chance to say goodbye to my family.

The marshals were nice to me and even admitted I got a raw deal. But still I was back at Terre Haute. Inmates were coming up to me and saying they couldn't believe the parole commission could do what they did. They said I had been the talk of the prison, and they all felt bad for me. Even some of the guards said they were sorry to see me back.

Because of all the controversy, I was returned to the main institution and wasn't allowed to be at the farm camp. But I got my old job back with Assistant Warden Lippman. He brought me into his office and told me that the only reason the parole board had rescinded my scheduled parole was because of the heat that the media put on them.

As soon as things settled down, I was able to think better. I would still have a chance to see the parole board, but I didn't expect anything to change.

As I was serving my time in Terre Haute, all hell was breaking loose back home, and many of my old friends were caught right in the middle. John Scalish, the longtime boss of the Cleveland Mafia, died, and there was a war for control of all the gambling. On one side was the new boss, Jack Licavoli, and on the other side were Danny Greene and John Nardi. John was a union official with ties to the mob. Danny Greene was a mob associate who was believed to have murdered

Charlie Broeckel's big-mouth friend, Shondor Birns.

During the war, my old friend Eugene Ciasullo, who was Licavoli's number-one enforcer, was almost killed by a bomb that was set off when he was approaching the front door of his house. I had only thought of explosives when it came to blowing safes. But now bombs were the main weapon being used to settle problems in the Cleveland mob.

It was a real embarrassment for Licavoli that two outsiders could get away with killing his underboss. But Licavoli's guys were having a lot of trouble trying to get Greene and Nardi. Pretty soon, two more of my old friends got involved in the war. Ronnie Carrabbia was Licavoli's street boss in Youngstown, and Ray Ferritto was called in because he had killed Julius Petro after it came out that Petro was a police informant in Los Angeles. I wondered if Petro's big mouth had blown our score at that private safe-deposit box company in L.A. back in 1971, but I'd never know.

In 1977, John Nardi was finally blown up. But the bomb wasn't planted on his car. It was put in a Joe Blow car, which was parked next to Nardi's, then detonated by remote control. The day of the murder, Danny Greene was interviewed on TV and called the Cleveland mob guys maggots. He even challenged them to come after him. A few months later, Butchie, Ronnie, and Ray killed Danny, using the same method. But they made a lot of mistakes, and Ray was arrested. When he found out that Licavoli was going to have him killed to keep him quiet, Ray made a deal with the authorities and testified against Ronnie and Butchie, who were sentenced to life. It was sad to hear because Ronnie and Ray had been as close to me as Charlie had been. But I soon had a serious problem of my own to deal with.

Chapter Twenty-Four

 It was now two months since I was back in Terre Haute, and I was getting tired easily and coughing a lot. Then one day I coughed up a mouthful of blood. I was put in the hospital. There were only two other inmates there, but they were kept separate since they had hepatitis. The doctor X-rayed my chest and saw what he thought was a tumor the size of a silver dollar on my left lung. When I heard tumor, I was thinking cancer. I thought to myself, what else is going to go wrong? But I was determined to stay strong. I wasn't going to let this defeat me.

When it was time for me to go in front of the Parole Board, the guards came for me with a wheelchair and had me wear a mask. But unfortunately I had no luck. The parole board came up with some bullcrap about how they'd been unaware of the ongoing criminal enterprise I was supposedly involved in when they originally agreed to give me parole. If they had known then of my association with the mob or that I was an unindicted co-conspirator in the burglaries involving the two Cleveland police supervisors that Charlie had ratted out, they would not have said yes to parole in the first place. Those are the reasons they cited, but I knew it was because of the controversy the newspaper reporter had started. They said I was a special case because I was considered a member of organized crime and was involved in a unique crime that got a lot of public attention. They also said I would not get another hearing for two years.

There was nothing left to do. My attorney said he'd file an appeal, but I knew that would take forever.

A few days later, the prison doctor sent me to the hospital section at the federal prison in Lexington, Kentucky. I'd heard of it before, because it was a co-ed facility, but I was too sick to even think about women. I'd even heard there was an experimental medicine section there where inmates from other institutions would volunteer to be guinea pigs, probably for a sentence reduction. Eventually the federal government outlawed that.

I was transported to Lexington on a prison bus and put in quarantine as soon as I arrived. A few days later, I was told I had tuberculosis, not a tumor. Naturally, I was very relieved it wasn't cancer. I was put on medication, and after another week I was released from quarantine and put in a room with another guy. This was much more like a hospital room than Terre Haute. After three weeks I was feeling better and getting my strength back, and so I was allowed to leave my room and move into the general population. The first day I went into the main population, I found it quite different than the prison life I was used to. Women and men doing time together!

At first I sat by myself and didn't talk to anybody. I liked looking things over first. But as the days went by and I felt better, I started meeting people and mingling with the crowd. If the guys in Terre Haute could have seen me, they would have flipped out. I met a young Mexican girl named Chickie, who was very pretty with jet black hair, brown eyes, and a nice little body. She started hanging around me and introducing me to her friends. They were all in couples and called each other their walkies because that's all you would see them doing. Men walking around with women. Almost everyone had a walkie. What a way to do time.

One day I was sitting in the dining hall eating with Chickie when this beautiful blonde inmate came toward us. I'd noticed her before walking around with different guys. She came right up to me and extended her hand.

"Since Chickie won't introduce us, I thought I'd introduce myself. I'm Irene."

"I'm Phil," I said, shaking her hand.

"Glad to meet you, Phil. See you around."

She left, and I could tell that Chickie was watching me look at her walk away.

"She's a fuckin' bitch," Chickie said.

"Why do you say that?"

"She thinks she's hot shit."

I could tell Chickie was jealous, which I could understand because Irene was gorgeous.

"What is she in for?"

"I don't know," Chickie said. Then she got up and stormed away.

Later that day I looked around for Chickie to see if she wanted to go see the movie that I'd heard they were showing in the auditorium. I couldn't find her but did see some guys I met and was getting friendly with, so I went with them. The movie was Jaws, and it was intense. I was so totally engrossed in the movie that when someone tapped me on the shoulder, I almost jumped out of my skin. It was Chickie. She smiled, and I asked her where she had been.

"Come with me," she whispered.

I got up and followed her to the back of the auditorium where there were only a few inmates. We sat down and were watching the movie for a few minutes when she leaned close to me and put her hand on my crotch. I started getting hard immediately. She smiled at me and started unzipping my fly. Then she started stroking me, and I could feel my heart pounding. My eyes were closed and rolling back in my head.

"Watch for guards," she said.

Then she leaned over in my lap and went down on me. I felt like I was sweating bullets. Let me tell you, it is a feat to watch for guards while getting a blow job. It didn't take me long to come, and I had to grit my teeth to keep from moaning. My whole body trembled. I was so relaxed and drained of energy that I could have just fallen asleep right there.

Not long after that, I heard they were having a dance in the gym, so I went with Chickie. The lights were dim and the music loud. I couldn't believe this was going on. For a while I was just standing around with Chickie, watching everybody dance and laughing because they were doing the Bump. I'd heard of it before, but this was the first time I saw it.

Suddenly someone grabbed my hand and jerked me out on the floor. It was Irene.

"I've never danced the Bump before," I shouted.

"There's nothing to it."

I was laughing as we danced, and I thought to myself that the guys at Terre Haute wouldn't believe it even if they could see me. When the music stopped, I went back where I'd been standing before. I looked around for Chickie but didn't see her. I figured she got mad and left, but I stayed at the dance and had a good time with Irene. We talked for a long time, and I found out she was from the West Side of Cleveland and used to be a model. She liked to smoke marijuana and got two years for smuggling cocaine into the country. It was the same thing Chickie was in for.

I didn't see Chickie around for a few days, so I was going on walks with Irene. She was telling me about the drug business and wanted me to get high with her. You could get marijuana easily at Lexington, but I told her I didn't smoke dope. Then one day she said she wanted to play shotgun. I said, "What in the hell is shotgun?" I thought it had something to do with sex. But she explained it was when a marijuana smoker blows smoke in someone's mouth. I tried it a couple of times but never got anything out of it. Then Irene told me about Seven-Fourteens, which were Quaaludes. I was getting quite an education in illegal drugs.

Two days later I finally ran into Chickie in the dining hall. I asked her where she had been.

"I thought you wanted to be with that blonde bitch."

"I was with you, and she just asked me to dance."

She didn't say anything else, but I could see she had an attitude about nothing. I just left and let her sulk in her own brew.

After that, I heard about a birthday party being held for one of the inmates. I went and found Irene there. She was higher than a kite and asked me if I wanted a Seven-Fourteen, but I said no. She got close to me and was rubbing her body against me. Then she walked over to some people and whispered something to them. She came back, took my hand, and walked me over to some accordion doors. Then she pulled them open. It was a closet.

"What are you doing?" I said.

"They'll jigger for us," she said, while glancing back toward her friends.

I just looked at her because I didn't know what she was talking about.

"They'll watch out for us. C'mon."

I thought to myself, this fucking broad is nuts. But I guess I was too because into the closet we went, and I helped her close the doors. She undid my pants fast, and a second later I was holding her by the cheeks of her ass as she reached down to guide me. She had her legs wrapped around me and was getting banged against the wall. It wasn't long before I exploded in pleasure. I wanted to just melt to the floor, but I knew we had to get out of there before we got caught. I opened the doors a little, peeked out, and we returned to the party. There were about twenty people who saw us come out of the closet, and they were all smiling at us. I felt like the cat that swallowed the mouse.

It didn't take long for everyone on the compound to find out. Including Chickie. The next day I was sitting in the dining hall eating with three other guys when she came storming in. She marched right up to our table and went off on me.

"So I hear you were fuckin' the mother-fuckin' blonde whore bitch in front of everybody!" she screamed. "You ain't gonna make a fool outta of me. You can have her!"

She turned and stomped away. Everyone had stopped talking and eating, and they all were looking me. I was totally embarrassed but tried to laugh it off.

"I guess she can't take a joke," I said to the inmate next to me.

But I was thinking to myself, that little mother-fucking Mexican cunt. She had better stay away from me. Then I had to laugh. It was like a scene from Peyton Place.

Chickie stayed away, and Irene became my walkie. We would walk together or find a quiet spot to sit. If there were no guards around, she would want to hold my hand.

So far Lexington had been a real trip, but there were even more surprises. On the Fourth of July, I was outside watching the guys and girls play softball. Suddenly I heard a whole pack of firecrackers go off from the inside compound dormitory. There was a guard leaning against a fence about forty feet away from me. He glanced over at the dorm, then went right back to watching the game. I couldn't believe this joint.

Another time I was on the inside compound and could smell marijuana smoke. It was pretty heavy, and a guard was passing by.

He turned to me and said, "Smells like good shit."

Then one time I was sitting in the outside compound with Irene. It was warm that day and the sun was out. Irene pointed toward a black food-service employee who worked for the Bureau of Prisons. The guy had on a very bulky jacket, and Irene said he was stealing food from the institution. I couldn't believe it. Right in broad daylight.

While in Lexington, I had a couple of visits. We were allowed to have food brought in, and when my family came, they brought a cooler full of stuff. My mother couldn't get over the place. She would ask me who were the prisoners and who were the visitors since we could wear our own clothes.

I was starting to get bored, though, and I was also thinking that I would probably get in trouble with these broads if I stayed there any longer. I was doing too much time to screw around and get a disciplinary violation. That would hurt me at my next parole hearing. It was great getting laid, but I thought it would be best for me to get back to the big house. I didn't tell Irene or any other inmates my intentions.

I was seeing the prison doctor once a week because he was monitoring my condition. I'd lost a lot of weight—down to one hundred fifty from one hundred seventy-five pounds. The doctor would do a quick exam, but all he really wanted to do was talk about the Mafia and my crimes. He was fascinated with that shit. The next time I saw him, I asked about going back to Terre Haute.

"Why? Don't you like this place, Phil?"

"Yeah, I like it doc but I'm doing too much time, and I'm scared I'll get in trouble with these broads."

"I understand," he laughed. "Yeah ,Phil, I'll put the paperwork in to release you. Just make sure you take the medication I prescribed."

About a week later, Irene came up to me. She looked sad.

"I have a friend who works in Receiving and Discharge," she said. "He saw your name, and you're being transferred back to Terre Haute."

Her eyes were welling up with tears. I acted surprised.

"Hey, don't be sad," I said. "We'll write and keep in touch, then we'll get together when we get out."

That seemed to brighten her up a little.

A few days later, she threw a big going-away party for me. I was getting a little high from all the marijuana smoke drifting around when Irene grabbed my hand and said, "Let's go for a walk." Before we left she talked to a couple of her friends. They followed behind us as we headed toward the gym. Irene told me they'd jigger. There was a bathroom with a door on it off the gym. We went in and wedged a chair under the doorknob. It looked safe enough.

Irene took her top off and pushed me toward the toilet where I sat down. She bent over and put her tits in my face. I sucked on her nipples for a few seconds as she was undoing her pants. She took them off quickly as I unzipped my pants. Then she put her legs on both sides of me and straddled me. Irene closed her eyes and was moving around and starting to get into it. My heart was beating fast and I was starting to breathe deeply.

Suddenly someone banged hard on the door twice, which jolted us back to reality. I figured it was Irene's friends. We both looked at the door, but there was silence.

"Who is it?" I said.

"It's Officer McNabb. Open the door."

Irene got off me, and I zipped my pants up.

"Open the door now," the guard said again sternly.

I held the door closed while Irene got dressed. I got a sick feeling in my stomach that this was happening. Where in the hell was the couple who were supposed to be jiggering for us? But it turned out that the guard's bark was worse than his bite. He gave us a tongue-lashing but didn't write us up. I never forgot his name because we got nabbed.

While Irene and I were walking away, we wondered where her friends had gone. But we found them still watching out for us. The guard had come up the stairs using a stairwell we didn't know about. It was a close call, and now I knew I had to get out of there.

A week later I was back at Terre Haute. I told my friends about Lexington, and they thought I was nuts for wanting to come back.

My old job in the assistant warden's office was filled, but I got an even better job in the captain's office. The other two inmates who worked in the captain's office were good friends from Chicago, and they wanted another good guy in the office. We worked for a guy named Mr. Tracey. He was a great person, and we all got along well.

The three of us had important jobs. One of the guys worked directly with the lieutenants, who were in an adjoining office. The other guy typed a lot of memos and did other office jobs the lieutenants needed done. He was also responsible for job assignments for all the guards in the prison. If we didn't like a guard, we would try our hardest to get him assigned to the towers. The guards hated tower assignment.

I was the T&A man. A lot of guys thought that was the perfect title for me after hearing about Lexington. But actually it stood for Time and Attendance. I was the clerk responsible for logging the number of hours that the guards, their supervisors, the counselors, and case managers worked. I recorded the actual times of the day that the guards worked because they got paid more for working at night. I also documented annual leave and sick time usage for all of these employees. Every second Sunday I'd be up late adding up the hours for each individual employee. Then the forms got sent to the finance office so the employees could get paid.

Once in a while, if there was an employee that I didn't like or that one of my friends didn't like, I'd purposely make a mistake on his payroll. Of course, I would make sure he got shorted, and it would take a month for the mistake to get corrected. Once in a great while, I would give one of my favorite guards a little overtime. I didn't do this very often and knew how to cover it if it was discovered. The guards weren't allowed to give us anything. But once in a while, they would "forget" a bag in the office, and the three of us would take it. It might be a bottle of vodka, cigarettes, or a special food item.

There were a lot of benefits working for the captain. When new guards were hired, I had to show them how to fill out the payroll forms. So I'd get to know them right away. I also had unlimited access to the office if I needed to do work. A guard could be walking by late at night, and if I asked, he would unlock my cell so I could go to the captain's office. Sometimes it would be to watch a good program on the television there. Or I'd ask the guard to get me the kitchen keys from the control room. Then we would see what looked good in the butcher shop. If I liked something, I would take it for the captain's office where there was a refrigerator and freezer, an electric skillet, and microwave oven. I even had my own secret storage space where I would stock up on tuna fish and sardines. Every time I went to the kitchen, I'd grab a few cans. And of course, I kept a few goodies in my cell, where I had a homemade Styrofoam cooler that I kept under my bunk.

Working with the payroll gave me a lot of clout. I did a good job and even won the Inmate of the Month award from the warden. I got a coffee cup with my name on it and twenty five dollars deposited into my account. And the local newspaper did a little write-up. Big deal.

I also helped inmates whenever I could, unless the guy was an asshole. Sometimes I could even discourage the lieutenant from putting an inmate in the hole. I helped one prisoner get transferred to another institution so he could be closer to home. We even got one guard fired. It took us a few months, but we did it. He thought he was a supercop and was always snooping around in the captain's office and searching through our desks. So along with my two other friends, we had a lot of power for inmates. And I played it to the hilt. Guys in other institutions heard I was damned near running the joint and wanted to get transferred here.

Every single guard knew who I was, and many of them wanted to do me favors. One of them was Officer Rodriquez, who was a really good guy. I nicknamed him Pork Chop because every time we went to the kitchen, he'd be looking for pork chops.

One Christmas Eve I was in the kitchen with Pork Chop. I told him I was going to be getting a lot of stuff because all the guys in my block were having a Christmas party. He said he didn't care as long as the lieutenant didn't mind. I told Pork Chop the lieutenant didn't care, but actually I'd never talked to him about it.

I got a big box and put in all kinds of lunch meat. Then I went to the vegetable room and got tomatoes, onions, celery, and lettuce.

"Let's go to the warehouse," I told Pork Chop.

"Warehouse? That box is full to the top already. How much more do you want?"

"I need more stuff from the back. C'mon."

Before we went to the warehouse, I got two big blocks of cheese, olives, pickles, ketchup, mayonnaise, mustard, tuna fish, bread, and buns. We covered the boxes with some old newspapers. Now I had three boxes filled with food for our party. I had one on my shoulder and was dragging the other one. I told Pork Chop to carry the other one.

"Phil, you're going to get both of us in trouble."

"Don't worry, you trembler."

"Okay, but if the lieutenant see us, he's gonna shit."

"Pick up the fuckin' box, Pork Chop. This is getting heavy."

He got the third box, and we walked through the dining hall and into the main corridor, which was totally empty. No guards were in the hall. Just as we were passing the lieutenant's office, the door opened. And there was the lieutenant. He saw the three boxes of food, then looked at me and Officer Rodriquez.

"What's going on here?" he said.

"I needed a few things for our Christmas party."

"Just pretend I didn't even see you," he said and walked away, shaking his head.

"You got me in trouble for sure," Pork Chop said.

I could see from the expression on his face that he was really nervous. But I knew I could straighten out this lieutenant because he and I would sit around at night and bullshit.

"Don't worry. I'll take the heat."

We got to the cell block, and Pork Chop went back to his post. The cell block guard unlocked the door for me.

"What's all this?" he said.

"It's just a few supplies I need for the office."

"Sure it is, Phil."

The guard opened my cell door, and I put the boxes on my bunk.

When I lifted the newspaper off he said, "Oh, shit."

"That is a mirage," I told him.

He stood there with his hands on his hips, shaking his head while I put the meat and cheese in my cooler.

"Boy, Christopher, the things you get away with."

"Hey, let me out again, I've got to go back to the office."

"Yeah, okay, but bring me back a steak dinner, medium rare."

"There's plenty here," I said, motioning toward the cooler and boxes. Make yourself a sandwich if you're hungry."

The guard's joke about a steak dinner was on my mind as I made my way back to the office. We didn't get steak often, but we had an excellent way of cooking it. It could be the toughest steak, but when you cooked it our way, it was like nothing you ever ate. We would put the steak in a small plastic bag and add seasonings and maybe some sliced onion. We'd suck all the air out of the bag with a straw and tie it so no air could get back in. After we plugged the drain in our cell sink, we'd turn on the hot water, which ran very hot.

The sinks had push-button faucets that you had to hold down to keep the water flowing. But for a pack of cigarettes, an inmate with the plumbing department would convert it to a regular valve. It was well worth it.

We'd wrap a small rag around the bag, put it in the bottom of the sink, and weigh it down with something heavy. The water pressure had to be adjusted just right so it filled the sink and ran out the overflow slowly. The steak would cook in its own juices and be done in about two hours. You'd open the bag, and the smell was mouthwatering. You could never believe how tender and delicious the meat was until you tasted it.

I had to get steak off my mind so I could straighten out the lieutenant for Pork Chop. When I reached the office, I found the lieutenant and told him I'd lied to Officer Rodriquez and to please not be mad at him since it was my fault. He said not to worry, he wasn't mad at Rodriguez, but he wanted me to dispose of the food as soon as possible. I told him no problem.

The next day was Christmas, and the party started in the afternoon. I brought out all the food and arranged it on five tables, and everyone started eating. There were about one hundred forty guys in our cell block, and one by one, they brought some of their own food that was brought in from the streets, which was allowed during the Christmas season. Hardly anyone on our block went to the chow hall that day because there was a ton to eat. It was a great party, with all nationalities celebrating Christmas together.

The guards never came in the back, but they knew what we were doing. Christmas was the most special day of the year, and they weren't going to bother us. Occasionally they'd look in from the front to make sure things were running smoothly.

The next day our party was the talk of the institution. But someone must have been jealous because a few days later I went to work and my boss looked very upset.

"What's wrong, Mr. Tracey?"

"Phil, the warden was snooping around in here. He found all that meat in the refrigerator, and now he's on the war path. And now the captain is upset with everyone."

I stood there shaking my head. Someone must have ratted on us. Between the other two inmate workers and me, we had twenty pounds of ground meat and sixty pounds of steaks in the freezer.

"I hope you guys don't have any more food in here," Mr. Tracey said.

He was looking at me, and I didn't answer right away.

"Phil, please, if you have anything else in here, get it out of here tonight."

"Okay, boss."

That evening I went to the office and to my secret hiding spot. It was a space at the bottom of a cupboard in the captain's office. All I had to do was pull up one board at the bottom. Over the months I had stacked about two hundred cans of tuna fish and sardines there. I went to the lieutenant on duty and told him I needed a cart from the kitchen. He said what for, and I told him we needed to bring some stuff to the kitchen. He wanted to see what it was and just pointed toward our office. When he saw all those cans of tuna and sardines, his eyes nearly popped out of his head. He told me I was going to get all the employees in the office fired. Then he called on the walkie-talkie for a guard to get the kitchen keys. I loaded all the tuna fish on a cart while the lieutenant watched and just shook his head. He told me to cover the cans, so I threw some old files on the top. Then the guard came, and we took the cart to the kitchen.

While we were walking, the guard asked me what I had, and I told him a bunch of tuna fish. He asked why I was taking it back. I explained and he laughed. I laughed to myself, thinking about all the trips I'd made to get this stuff, and now I was bringing it all back.

The next day when I came to work, Mr. Tracey said he'd heard about my venture and thanked me for taking care of business.

"Where the hell did you have all those tuna and sardines?" he asked.

But then he put his hand up and said, "No, don't tell me. I don't want to know. But why did you have so much?"

"Boss, you never know when there's going to be a nuclear war."

Chapter Twenty-Five

It was 1978, and I had been back at Terre Haute two years. One day I came back from lunch, and Mr. Tracey said my lawyer, Howard Siegrist, had called for me and would call back soon. I thought that was unusual and couldn't imagine what was up. I waited, and the phone rang. The other guys and the captain were watching as Mr. Tracey motioned for me to come over and gave me the phone. Howard told me he had some good news. I was going to be paroled in two months. I couldn't believe it because I really wasn't expecting a break and was just doing my time. I'd totally forgotten about the street. I was so excited I could have kissed Howard. Everyone was happy and congratulated me.

I went back to my desk, but it was hard to concentrate. I just had to tell my parents, but when I called my mother, she told me that Howard had already called them. She said that at least I wouldn't have to worry about the halfway house because I would just be paroled to the street. It hadn't even occurred to me to ask Howard about a halfway house.

The two months went by fast. I said goodbye to everyone, and the guys in my cell block gave me a huge party. Even inmates from other cell blocks were there. Everyone said it was the biggest going-away party they had ever seen at Terre Haute.

When I got to my parents' house, my son was there. He lived with his mother just down the street from my parents. I had only seen him once in six years, and he was a teenager now. At that age and with me having been gone so much, it was hard to talk with him. He was quiet, but that's the way I always was when I met someone new.

I thought Maggie would stop over, but she didn't. I called her on the phone, and we got together a few days later. I could just tell she didn't feel the same about me.

It felt so good to be on the street again. A good friend of mine got me a job with this construction company that did underground utility work-water lines, sanitary and storm sewers. The guys in the field made very good money, but I was still too weak from TB to do any construction work. I'd gained all of my weight back but not my strength. So I was basically a gofer for the owner. He gave me a station wagon to use, and I ran all kinds of errands for him. He was totally legit but liked the idea of hanging around with someone who was associated with the mob.

There were these elaborate dinners on Tuesday nights at the Italian-American Brotherhood Club, or the IAB Club, in Little Italy, that my boss wanted me to go to with him a few times. At the time they were hosted by Carmen Milano, whose father Tony had been the Cleveland Mafia's *consigliere*, or counselor. Jack Licavoli lived in Little Italy and was often at the dinners, which drew construction and other business owners, politicians, and even judges. I think my boss attended because it made him feel important. He was always after me to go. I did go a few times, but to me it was all a bunch of bullshit and wannabes. But I kept my thoughts to myself and gave everybody respect, especially the older guys.

Once in a while, I would talk to Jack Licavoli when nobody was kissing his ass. One Tuesday evening he came up and asked me to see him in Carmen's office. My boss waited outside.

As soon as I closed the office door, Jack said, "It's good to get away from all those suck-asses."

It made me laugh because that's what I thought they were too.

"Phil, you're a good boy," Jack said. "I like what I hear about you. You're quiet and you know how to make money. I'd like you to come and work for me. You don't have to answer right now, but think about it and let me know."

"I appreciate the offer, Jack. I'll think about it."

That night my boss asked me what Jack wanted, but I told him I'd rather not say. He said he understood. We stopped at a bar after we left the IAB Club, and it was just like I thought it would be with him. He wanted to be so like a gangster. He asked me question after question about how I got started in crime. Then he told me to keep the station wagon I had been using to run errands because I didn't have a car yet. And he said I could use his credit card to get gas. What a score that was.

While I was working for the construction company and getting myself reestablished on the streets, my relationship with Maggie ended. I wanted to get married, but she said she couldn't do it. She was afraid that someday I'd wind up back in prison.

Then I met a cocktail waitress named Diane. It turned out she used to drink with her girlfriends at the Redwood, but I didn't remember her. Having just been released from prison, I was only looking for one thing, and so before long Diane and I were sleeping together. But only a few months later, we got married.

I bought a corner house that was right next door to a store owned by a cousin of mine. I needed more money to live, so I asked my boss if I could work in the field. He told me the work was hard, but that didn't bother me. I got my strength back and wasn't afraid of working hard, if I really had to. I started doing underground utility construction. But it still wasn't enough money for me, so I brought my burglar tools back out. I knew the risk involved, but I just put it out of my mind. When it came to wanting big money, I was addicted.

I went to Youngstown to hook up with some of my old friends in the business and get back in the game. I got in touch with Joe DeRose, an organized crime figure and burglar who was close with Ronnie Carrabbia, and he introduced me to a few of his friends. They had heard of me and knew of my reputation, but these guys weren't doing many burglaries anymore. The new thing was marijuana. But I didn't know anything about it and didn't want to sell drugs. They told me if I was interested to call them. I told them if I found a good score I'd let them know.

I'd been thinking about Jack Licavoli's offer to work with him. But I knew what would happen. I didn't want people telling me what to do. I liked being my own man. And furthermore, a lot of the people who were around Jack turned my stomach. There were phonies and wannabe gangsters.

"I appreciate your offer," I said to Jack. "But I prefer not to change my working arrangements."

"I'm sorry to hear that, Phil, but if you ever change your my mind, the offer still stands."

Then I called my old friend Frank who used to work with ADT. I figured Charlie Broeckel had probably ratted him out, so I was surprised when he told me he was still with ADT. He said the feds did talk to him after Charlie flipped, but he just denied everything. He never got in any trouble and didn't lose his job. After all those years, Frank was still hurting for money, so I told him we'd go back to work. He liked that, and a few days later, he gave me a list of jewelry stores and alarm specs for each one. I recognized one as a big diamond dealer called Wholesale Jewelers.

The only bad thing was that it was in Beachwood, a wealthy, eastside suburb with good police coverage. If the score wasn't done right, it could be a death trap. I asked Frank to find out what kind of alarms they had, and I decided to watch the building myself to see how often the law rolled the building, which was four stories high and had a lot of different business offices and a fancy restaurant inside.

The next day I met with Frank, and he told me the card for Wholesale Jewelers showed two alarms with ADT but additional coverage by Honeywell, another big security company. Frank explained that things had changed since I'd been gone. The insurance companies were now requiring some businesses to use two separate alarms. I thanked Frank and told him I'd call if I needed anything else.

That weekend I met Joe DeRose in Cleveland. Skinny Sam Fossesca came too.

I told them about the Wholesale Jewelers score and Joe said he wanted to bring two guys—his friend Dick Hinkel from Pittsburgh and this other guy who had a burning bar. I thought that was a good idea, because we didn't know what kind of safe was in there. The burning bar, a powerful cutting torch, heats to ten thousand degrees and will go through just about anything. Nobody had ever heard of it in the burglary scene until I started using it for certain scores. The first time I used it was in the sixties while I was in somebody's garage trying to open a safe we'd just grabbed. When I ignited the rod, I was startled by the enormous amount of light and smoke. The sparks put holes in my shoes and pants and started a fire in the garage. We managed to put the fire out but had to buy protective clothing from a welding store to finish the job.

I told Joe I'd bring the oxygen and acetylene tanks, torch, gauges, walkie-talkies, and police scanner. Sam said he'd bring the alarm boxes. We set the date for a Saturday two weeks away and arranged to meet in a parking lot across from the Wholesale Jewelers score. That weekend and the next Saturday, I checked out the area for police coverage. No cops came through the lot, and everything looked good.

The day of the score, I was a little tense because this was my first score in seven years or so. We decided that Joe, Sam, and I would go in. Dick Hinkel would drop us off, then park in the lot while monitoring the police scanner and the walkie-talkie. Dick Hinkel gave me bad vibes. He was quiet, and there was just something about him I didn't like.

We walked to the side entrance, which was open because of the restaurant in the building. Sam was carrying a small suitcase. We went into the phone room on the second floor, and Joe stood guard. Sam took out his alarm boxes, which were an updated style because of the new alarm technology. I watched him work and understood everything he was doing. I was thinking that as soon as I got some money, I would get some of those boxes. The alarm was ready to be jumped out. Sam switched the boxes on, and it was time for us to back off.

We walked out of the building pretty fast, got in the car, and I told Dick to drive across the street to another parking lot. We waited there and listened to the police scanner. Fifteen minutes later there had been no alarm broadcast, so we drove back over to the score.

Sam and I got to the jewelry store door and started working on prying it open with the L-bar. I used a big screwdriver to find a small opening between the door and the frame so that Sam could get the bar in. The door popped right open, and I hit the tongue of the lock with the sledgehammer so it would go in and the door could close.

We were in. Sam and I both put on masks in case there were surveillance cameras filming. We got out penlights and looked around the main room, but there were no safes there. Then I heard Joe whisper for us. I told him to come in but to stand guard by the glass door. Joe took the walkie-talkie.

Sam and I opened a door to another room and found two safes. We closed the door so we could put the light on since there were no windows in that room. After checking to make sure there were no surveillance cameras, we took our masks off. I was sweating heavily.

One of the safes was a newer one, and the other one was older. I tried to turn the handle of the older one because you never know. It was locked. Sam and I opened the old safe in no time and found a little bag filled with diamond rings. We figured the good shit was in the new safe, so I got to work on that.

I set up the acetylene torch. There was no carpeting on the floor, so I didn't have to worry about a fire. I squeezed the striker, lit the torch, and started burning. I was putting the heat to it and watching for the metal to start flowing. Sam and Joe were watching intently, and I was waiting and waiting but nothing was happening. I stopped for a second and checked the gauges. Everything was set perfectly, so I tried again. But the safe wouldn't burn. We figured it was a new stainless steel, torch-resistant model. I stopped and turned the torch off. It was sure getting warm in that little room. Sweat was rolling down my face.

I said to Joe, "Where's the burning bar?"

"I didn't bring it," he said.

"You didn't bring it. What the fuck, Joe, you were supposed to bring it."

"Sorry, Phil. The guy who had it wasn't home."

Sam said, "Let's see if we can get a bite at the corner."

I was very agitated with Joe, but I thought to myself, maybe we can pop this safe open yet. I held a wedge in place at the corner, and Sam hit it with the sledgehammer. Sam was banging away, and the wedge was slowly moving in, but we were making a lot of noise.

Now that we had the wedge in, we got the railroad bar and tried to get the door open. The three of us maneuvered around the bar, grabbed a section, and were pushing and pushing. We stopped for a second, and I adjusted the tip. Again we grabbed the bar and pushed hard for a good minute. Finally we made a little progress. The door was open at the corner about a quarter inch.

We stopped to rest from all the exertion, and I took my penlight and shined it through the space in the door. There were a bunch of diamonds sparkling from the beam. And that was just in one corner of the safe. The other guys peeked in. Seeing those gems sure gave us some more energy to work with. We got in position again and went to work. After another minute I checked. We weren't making any progress.

"We need the burning bar," I said. "Sam, do you have any other ideas?"

He shook his head.

"Joe, can you go and get it?" I asked.

"Yeah, if the guy is home."

"Do you know where it's at?"

"In his garage."

"Well then go and get it."

"But the guy might not let me have it unless he comes on the score."

I knew from that remark that Joe had never even looked into getting the burning bar in the first place. But there was no sense in starting an argument on the score.

"Just tell him he can come, too," I said.

"Okay," Joe said. "Dick and I'll go."

Joe called on the walkie-talkie, "We're coming home."

I heard Dick answer, "I'll be there in two minutes."

We waited a few minutes to make sure he was there since we were carrying everything out. I was mad because we should have been done and going somewhere to cut up the loot.

I told Joe to go first and make sure nobody was standing around by the restaurant door. He went out, then motioned for us to come. The valet for the restaurant was sitting nearby but didn't notice us coming out with our bags of equipment. After we got in the car, I looked over to see if he was watching us. He glanced over but wasn't paying attention. Dick pulled away and commented that the score went fast. Joe said we weren't done and that we had to go get the burning bar from Sonny. I didn't know who Sonny was and I didn't care as long as we got the burning bar and got in to get those diamonds.

It was about 2:00 a.m., and we decided to get a room at a Holiday Inn, which was just down the road, so that we wouldn't be riding around or sitting in a parking lot and get questioned by the police. Dick got us a room, then he and Joe left for Youngstown. We figured they'd be gone about two hours. Sam and I went up to the room, and I plugged the police scanner into the room outlet to save the batteries. We watched TV and waited.

After about three hours, someone knocked on the door. I looked out the peephole and saw Joe, Dick, and some other guy, so I knew they had the burning bar. They came in with coffee and doughnuts, and Joe introduced me to Sonny, who was big and dirty-looking. I sure didn't like the idea of bringing someone I didn't know on a score, but we needed that burning bar. Joe said they'd brought about twenty feet of bar and two oxygen tanks.

We had our coffee and doughnuts, and it was just starting to get light. We decided to wait until daylight to finish the score because we'd look less suspicious than if we were seen going in the building at the crack of dawn.

Forty-five minutes later I looked out the window and the sky was clear. It was going to be a beautiful day. Just then something on the police scanner caught my attention. All it said was to check for a possible break-in at some location on Chagrin Boulevard. I had no idea of the jewelry shop address, but I knew Chagrin was a long street. And if it was our score, it would have been a big thing on the police radio. We were ready to go. I told Sam we should take a ride by the building first to see how everything looked. Everybody else could just wait there till we came back.

We got in my car and drove over and could see the building. Everything looked quiet as we approached it, but then we noticed two cop cars parked on the side. We figured we'd better go back to the room and grab the scanner. I drove back, parked the car, and Sam ran up to the room. Two minutes later he came out slowly. He was shaking his head and didn't have the scanner.

"What's wrong?" I said. "Where's the scanner?"

"We've been made, Phil."

"What do you mean?"

"We've been made. It's all over the scanner about a break-in and safe-opening at Wholesale Jewelers."

I couldn't believe it. I got out of the car and went up to the room with Sam. There was still chatter on the police radio about the jewelry store. I was fucking hot now. If Joe had remembered the burning bar the first time, this wouldn't have happened. We'd be home and asleep. And rich.

"We better get as far away from here as we can," I told Sam.

He said, "I'll take what we got and get rid of it for a good price."

"That's fine."

I jumped in my car and hit the freeway north as fast as I could. I was mad, but I thought at least we got something. But we didn't know how much we'd missed.

It wouldn't be long before we found out.

The next day Frank from ADT called me. He sounded hyper, like he was in some sort of trouble. He wanted to meet me right away at Manners Big Boy

Restaurant. When I pulled in the parking lot, he was standing outside. He looked all frustrated and disappointed.

"What the fuck happened?" he said.

"The law came and we had to leave."

"Christ, Phil. Do you know how much you missed?"

"I don't know."

"$1.4 million worth of diamonds."

That did make me sick. I had to laugh though, because Frank looked more upset than I was.

"Do you know how they found the score?" he said.

I had no idea, but it looked like Frank had all the answers that morning.

"No. Tell me."

"A fucking accountant came to get caught up on some work. He saw some white powder footprints coming from the office across the hall from his office, walked up to the door, pushed on it, and found it open. Then he called the police."

"That dirty mother-fucker," I said. The powder must have been from the first safe we opened.

Frank was disgusted. I was disgusted. But there was nothing we could do to change the facts.

"Well, we got one safe open," I told him. "At least we left with something."

"How come you didn't get the other safe open? I thought you're the best."

This mother-fucker has some balls asking that, I thought to myself.

"It wasn't my fault. One of the guys was supposed to bring the burning bar, but he forgot it."

"Jeez, Phil," he said, shaking his head. "How come you go with assholes?"

"What can I say? I can't do everything."

I could see he was really upset. Then he said he had to go. I had to laugh to myself again.

As he was leaving, he shook his head and said, "Boy, what I could have done with that money."

As he took off, I could see his dollar signs were going down the sewer.

The following week Joe DeRose called.

"I sold that car for you and have your money."

I knew what he meant.

"Great. I'll be up on Saturday."

We got a little over fifty thousand dollars for the Wholesale Jewelers stuff. I was surprised because I didn't think we would get that much. Joe gave me two packages—one for me and one for Frank. Then I told him what we'd missed and how the score was found out. He felt bad and said it was his fault that we didn't get the other safe.

Then Joe said he was working on a big score in Pittsburgh worth about $10 million in diamonds. He added that I was included in the score, which sounded great to me. He said he would get in touch with me a week before it came down.

On the way home, I was thinking that I didn't ask Joe what the total value of the score was. I figured there must have been about two hundred fifty thousand dollars worth of jewelry. I was also thinking that at least now I could get some of those new alarm boxes. Skinny Sam had told me he would introduce me to the friend who built them for him.

When I got home, I met with Frank to give him his cut. He looked paranoid.

"How much is there?" he whispered while peeking in the bag.

"Almost five thousand dollars."

He looked at me with delight and said, "Oh yeah."

Then he turned all serious and started to talk quietly out of the corner of his mouth. He even put his hand by his mouth as if to whisper in my ear. He made me laugh because he was so dramatic at times.

"You got a lot of heat for that job," he told me. "They called the FBI when they found those alarm jumping boxes. They said everything has been quiet around this area since you were in prison. Now that you're out, they believe you're back at work."

"And they're right," I said.

Frank looked around like somebody was watching him. Now he was starting to make me nervous.

"I am going to go," he said.

I laughed. "Okay, Frank."

He left, and I watched to see if by chance there was a tail on him. I even followed at a long distance as he went home, but I didn't see any tails.

Chapter Twenty-Six

I'd always been against selling drugs, and certainly I never used them. But every guy I knew in the drug business said the profits were easy and very big. Plus I already knew quite a few people who smoked marijuana and could be customers. And so I went back up to Youngstown to see a guy we called Tubby, an old burglar who'd lost his nerve. Tubby had the connection for the drugs and was part of a crew headed by Joey Naples. Naples had a vending machine company and was the Pittsburgh mob street boss in the area.

Tubby sold me some marijuana, and before I went back home, he said, "Joe DeRose is causing trouble. He's telling people he's going after Joey Naples and he's gonna take over Youngstown. A battle's brewing, Phil, and guys are choosing sides."

"That's their problem, Tub. All I want to do is make money. I fight my own problems, not other people's problems."

That was the reason I wouldn't go to work with Jack Licavoli. I wanted to be my own boss and not get involved in the mob power struggles.

I was surprised at how fast the marijuana sold, and I went back to Youngstown for more. Within a couple of months, I was making about a thousand dollars a week. The guys were right. It was easy money. Even though I'd been against it for a long time, I was now sold on the drug business. Like I always said, money was king.

I was still working construction and running back and forth to Youngstown to buy smoke. So I just kept a low profile when I came to Youngstown. Instead of hanging around all day, I would just get my smoke and make some excuse that I had to get right back to Cleveland.

One time I brought fifty pounds of marijuana back. It was raining hard and I had a leak in my trunk, so it got soaked. I needed somewhere to spread it out so it would dry. Diane and I lived next door to my cousin's vacant store, so I asked her if I could put some construction tools in it. I put newspapers all over the floor and spread the smoke out so it would dry. It had an awfully strong smell, but fortunately Diane never noticed.

Not long after I got into the marijuana business, a couple of Youngstown mob guys were murdered. In December 1978, Spider Grisham was shot by a sniper while he was at his front door, and in July of 1979, Jack Tobin was shot in his home.

It was maybe two or three months after Tobin's murder that I was in Youngstown to pick up some smoke. I stopped at Joe DeRose's apartment to say hi, and I could tell he was in another world, taking pills and boozing a lot. It was getting to his mind, and he was obsessed with talk about taking over Youngstown. Joe also brought up the murders of Grisham and Tobin and made laughing remarks. He wasn't actually saying he did it but was making it very easy to read between the lines.

I wanted nothing to do with it. I was just checking in with him to see what was going on because he and Skinny Sam were good friends. And I knew that sooner or later they would come up with a good burglary score.

About four to six months later, I went to Youngstown and stopped at Joe's apartment. It was about 9:00 a.m., and here was Joe drinking wine in his dining room with Dick Hinkel. Joe started talking about a million dollars of life insurance money that Dick was supposed to get from Lloyds of London because some girl that Dick had insurance on got killed. I really wasn't paying too much attention because I felt uneasy. I hate talking to people when they're drunk, and I didn't care for this Dick Hinkel.

Then Joe brought up the recent murder of John Magda. I knew Magda, but he was nothing but a nickel-and-dime thief. I'd heard he was found with his head wrapped in duct tape like a mummy.

"What do you think about Magda getting it, Phil?"

"Who would want to waste their time killing him? He couldn't hurt a fly," I said.

"He had a mouth that wouldn't stop. I wonder how he likes this around his face?" He smiled, holding up a roll of duct tape. "I bet it keeps his mouth closed now."

I thought to myself, I better get the fuck out of here.

Then guys in Naples's crew asked me if I wanted to come up to Youngstown and get something started. Naples needed protection against Joe DeRose and in exchange, we were going to get the local crap games. I didn't like the idea because I didn't know anything about gambling. But over the next few weeks, I thought about it. I knew there were big profits in gambling.

The next week an attempt was made to kill Joe DeRose. He and his girlfriend were shot but not hurt badly. I just shook my head. What in the world was going through Joe's mind, I thought. I guess he was trying to prove something to himself. I decided to take a ride to Youngstown to see how Joe was doing, but he wasn't at his apartment. Then I drove up to the used car lot where Naples's crew hung out. Tubby and some other guys had rented a store next to the lot and had a crap game going.

One of Naples's main guys asked me again if I wanted to stay in Youngstown and work for Joey Naples. "DeRose is out of control, Phil. Naples needs protection and says we can have the gambling, bingo, and numbers if we want it."

"That sounds good to me," I said.

"Why don't you hang out up here with us? What kind of expenses would you need?"

I thought it over for a minute and figured I'd better make up my mind now if I'm in. DeRose was a good friend, but he was out of line and would eventually be killed. And if I could get a piece of the gambling, I could make some real money.

"I'd need a place to live and five hundred dollars a week."

The guy said he'd be right back. While I waited, I sat around watching the crap game, bullshitting with Tubby, and eating some cold cuts they had for the players. A few minutes later, Naples's guy came over and said that he got the okay for the expense money and they would be renting an apartment for the bodyguards to stay in. He didn't say who he talked to, but I assumed it was Joey Naples.

And so I quit my construction job and was living mostly in Youngstown. We got a panel truck to move around in and had a portable arsenal to protect Joey Naples. We had an M-15, an M-1 carbine, and a couple of shotguns besides our own personal pistols.

Every day, a few of us would go down to where Joey Naples had his office. We would just sit around and bullshit. And every day I would say to myself, this money is the easiest money I've ever made. I wasn't doing anything but in reality, I was right in the middle of a Mafia war. Still it would be worth it when Joey Naples gave me a piece of the gambling in Youngstown.

Between the hours I worked in Youngstown and driving back and forth, it was starting to take its toll on Diane and me. Things were going okay for a while, but then I started having trouble with her, like the time one afternoon when I got home and told Diane to get dressed and grab her driver's license. She looked at me puzzled and asked where we were going.

"You're going to buy a gun." I was leaving my gun in Youngstown and wanted to have some legal firepower at home.

"A gun?"

"Yeah, a gun."

"Why do I need a gun?"

"I'll tell you on the way."

We got in the car and headed to a gun shop. I told Diane that if something happened at home and I needed a gun, I wanted it to belong to her. If my parole officer decided to search my house, at least I could say the gun was my wife's. I told Diane not to worry. I didn't believe anything would happen. I just wanted to be safe than sorry.

She got quiet. A few minutes later, she started on me.

"Phil, when are you ever going to slow down? You're here. You're there. You're trying to make money and fighting with different people you don't even know, for people you hardly know. I know what you're doing."

I thought to myself, where does she get this kind of information? I surely don't say anything, and nobody knows in this town what I'm doing up in Youngstown.

"I don't know where you get your information," I said. "But somebody is telling you a whole bunch of shit."

"You don't think I know that you had marijuana in your cousin's store?"

I couldn't believe she knew about that.

I said, "What the fuck are you talking about?"

"You know exactly what I'm talking about. It smelled real bad."

Fortunately we'd just pulled into the gun store parking lot.

Before we got out of the car, I said, "I want you to ask for a twelve-gauge pump shotgun. If he asks you what you want it for, just say it's for hunting."

"Phil, I'm not comfortable doing this."

"Don't worry. I'll be right there. Just go in and ask to see a twelve-gauge pump shotgun."

We went in and walked up to the counter, and the clerk asked how he could help us.

Diane said, "I want to see a twelve-gauge shotgun pump."

The guy glanced at me and smiled as he walked away.

"What's so funny?" Diane said.

"You said shotgun pump. It's pump shotgun. Don't worry about it. It's no big thing."

The clerk brought back a nice semi-automatic shotgun and a pump shotgun. He asked Diane what she was going to use for, and she said hunting. I was just standing beside her as he was showing her the two shotguns. Now that I saw the semi-automatic, I liked it better than the pump.

I nudged Diane's foot with mine and said, "Maybe this semi-automatic would be easier for you to fire."

She said, "I'll take this one," and pointed to the semi-automatic. Then he asked her if she needed shells. She looked at me, and I said I already had some. She showed him her driver's license, and before long we were on our way home. I felt a little more at ease, now that I had some firepower that was legal. Diane said she was glad that was over but then started complaining again about how I was out of town so much. I couldn't wait to drop her off at home. There were too many women in the world to have to always be bickering with your wife.

Back in Youngstown, I grabbed a couple of broads. The best place to go was on the strip in Warren. That town I liked. It reminded me of Cleveland and had some fine-looking women.

During one visit to Youngstown, I found out that a lot of the guys were getting out of the marijuana business. They told me that cocaine brought in more money and wasn't as bulky as smoke. It sounded good to me, but I knew nothing of the business and would have to look for customers.

It didn't take long because there was a big market in Cleveland. I started with some black guys I knew. Pretty soon I went from selling marijuana to selling cocaine. A few months later, I was making a bundle. At that rate I figured I could make a million, invest it in a legit business, and retire within a year.

During another trip to Youngstown, I got a message to call my wife. I was told it was an emergency. When I reached Diane, she said that my father had chest pains and felt dizzy. I told her to go over there and take him to the hospital. "What are you waiting for?" I said.

I jumped in the car and burned rubber all the way home. I hit the turnpike and went one hundred ten miles per hour. The rest of the highway I was going eighty-five miles per hour. I never knew how long it actually took me to get home because that was the furthest thing from my mind.

When I got to the hospital, my mother and brother told me that my father had had a heart attack. He was okay now and was resting. They were going to keep him in the intensive care unit.

I went in to see my dad, and he was sleeping. I asked the nurse how he was doing, and she said he'd a heart attack but was okay now. As I watched my father sleep, I couldn't help but think of all the pain I'd caused him and my mother over the years.

Chapter Twenty-Seven

In 1980, Youngstown was a bomb ready to explode now that Charlie Carrabbia disappeared. He was the main Cleveland mob guy since his brother Ronnie had been sent to prison for bombing Danny Greene, the Irishman who tried to take over the Mafia. Charlie's car was found in Cleveland. Then Junior Senzarino was killed. He was the first guy to show me how to drill a safe open. Tubby told me how he was killed. Junior had just pulled in his driveway and pushed his garage door opener. When the garage opened, he pulled the car in, but the killer snuck in behind him. After Junior closed the door, they blew him away with a shotgun. The only way out of the garage was through a window. The shooter jumped through and must have got cut because the police found a lot of blood outside the garage. The word was that Joe DeRose killed Junior because he beat him out of money from a diamond score.

Then in February of 1981, Joe DeRose's father was walking down his driveway to move a car when a gunman jumped out and fired a shotgun. Joe DeRose, Sr. was killed instantly. Later I learned that Joey Naples's crew was responsible. It was a case of mistaken identity, but it was a mistake I couldn't excuse. And so I got in touch with Naples's main guy and told him I didn't want to work for

Joey anymore.

In April, Naples won his war with Joe DeRose, Jr. Joe's car was found burned out near Akron, Ohio. He was presumed murdered, but his body was never found.

During 1981, several of my friends got out of prison, one right after the other. Of course, I gave them some money when they first got out. I told them how easy it was to make money in the drug business, but like me, they were mostly burglars and had never dealt with drugs before. They were bugging me to do some scores, but I told them selling drugs was easier.

I continued to make trips to Youngstown to pick up coke, but then the supplier ran out. I was never one to rely on others to make me money, so I went in partners with Mike, another guy I met in Youngstown. Mike had a connection in Florida, and he and I started getting our own coke.

Now that we'd eliminated the middleman, I was making even more money. I even went in partners on a body shop with a friend of mine named Billy O'Neal. I put up thirty thousand dollars and he ran it. Billy was a black guy I was very close with. I used him on a score in which he impersonated an armored car employee, walked into a bank and was given three hundred sixty thousand dollars. But he got caught and the money was recovered. Billy did his time and never ratted anyone out.

By now my marriage to Diane had deteriorated to the point where I moved out. I started renting a three-bedroom apartment on the tenth floor of the Gates Mills Towers, a pretty plush apartment complex on the East Side. A few weeks after I moved in, I met Jackie Presser, who also lived in the complex. He was the president of the Teamsters Union and was a very powerful figure who was well-connected with the Cleveland mob. I'd see Jackie now and then, and he'd want to talk. He'd mention that he had a few ideas for us to make some money, but for some reason I didn't trust him. One time he brought up drugs, but I told him I didn't like them.

During this time, I met an eighteen-year-old blonde named Sue and started going out with her. I was thirty-six but felt a lot younger. I bought her a car, then got myself a twenty-four-foot cabin cruiser. I started water skiing, and if Sue was busy I'd drive my boat down to the Flats, a big entertainment area near downtown Cleveland, and party until the sun came up. Sometimes I drank so much that I didn't know how I drove the boat back and docked it. When winter came, I took up snow skiing. I was having a ball.

Meanwhile those friends of mine who'd just got home from prison were really pressing me to make a move. And so we hit a couple of jewelry stores and made a nice buck. But it seemed like I always had a tail, sometimes several cars, so I was being very careful.

Around that time I started watching a department store called Clarkins. They were having a big going-out-of-business sale, and there was supposed to be a hundred thousand in cash in four safes. That sounded good to me for one night's work.

Clarkins sat real nice, with some quiet side streets and railroad tracks behind it that we could use to approach the store. The telephone cables ran underground, which meant we'd have to disable the alarm from the inside. The loading dock area had a canopy that we could use to get onto the roof. There was a bowling alley across the street.

I had crew of five guys, including an old friend, Deacon Conte. Every night a couple of us would go in before closing and check things out. We saw where the office and safes were, along with the telephone box. The best thing was that there were no overnight security guards.

On the night of the score, we watched from the bowling alley lot until everyone left. We double-checked to make sure all the employees were out by calling the store to see if anybody answered. When we were sure everyone was gone, we drove to one of the side streets and parked. Then we walked through some high brush and weeds and across the railroad tracks until we came to the back of the store. We put all our equipment bags down and took a rest while we monitored the police scanner.

One of the guys stayed on the ground as a lookout. We had walkie-talkies to communicate. The rest of us used a small stepladder to get onto the canopy.

From there, we got on the roof.

The roof was flat and covered with gravel. We scraped the gravel out of the way and pulled up the tar paper. There was about eight inches of Styrofoam under that, and we pulled it, then got to the wood. Then we used our big six-foot wrecking bar and pried up some of the boards until we had a good-sized hole to drop in.

We had a rope that was knotted every foot or so. I tied it around my waist and put my penlight in my mouth. Then I dropped down into the darkness while the guys held the other end of the rope.

I eased down until my feet hit a dropped ceiling. I kicked a couple of the tiles out of the way and lowered myself down to the floor. It was dark, but it looked like I was in some kind of office. I glanced up, and Deacon was watching me. Then I looked around. There was a big table and vending machines. I was in an employee lunchroom. I looked up and told Deacon that everything was okay, and he dropped down my bag of alarm tools.

I walked out of the lunchroom, past the checkout and counter to the office. I used a big screwdriver to pop the doorknob lock. I was listening just in case Deacon called to me. I flipped the light switch on and went right to the telephone box. Then I pulled the cover off and noticed the little tags the security companies use to label the alarm wires. I laughed to myself and wondered if they knew how easy they made it for burglars.

I reached into my bag for my alarm box when I heard something and looked up toward the door. I froze for a second. I couldn't believe it, but there were two security guards aiming shotguns at me. My first thought was that I'd been set up.

One guard yelled, "Don't move or I'll blow your head off."

I could see that he was more nervous than I was, so I didn't move. I could hear Deacon and the other guys scrambling off the roof.

The guard told me to lie on my stomach. I did, and he handcuffed me, then told me to stand up. He asked me how I got in, but I didn't answer. The other guy wasn't saying anything. They made me walk to the front of the store, but they weren't aiming their guns at me and I was looking around for a way to escape. If I had been handcuffed in the front, I might have been able to throw something through the front windows.

The guard made me sit down, then he called the police. I was hoping that Deacon and the other guys got away. While the guard was talking on the phone, I realized that the other guard wasn't a guy but a girl. Now I was even more disgusted. When the male guard hung up, he asked me again how I got in. I was feeling cocky.

"I walked through the wall."

He said, "You spicks think you're so tough, don't you?"

I just laughed at him. He was trying to be a tough guy in front of the girl. There were sirens in the distance and then got louder. A minute later, the police were knocking on the door but the security guards didn't have a key to let them in. I was upset I got grabbed, but this was like a three-ring circus.

I was relaxed now and just trying to make the best of it.

I told the guard, "If you take the cuffs off, I'll get that door open for you."

"Just keep your mouth shut, wise guy."

It was about forty-five minutes before they got the store manager down to unlock the door. The regular cops had left, and now two detectives came in. They told the guards that they'd checked the roof and found where I'd come in. They added that anyone else involved had got away. I was glad to hear that.

The detective came over, asked my name, and I told him. He turned to his partner and said, "We're arresting one of the best burglars around."

There wasn't much more said between us. But then I heard something that made me sick. The male security guard mentioned to the detectives that this was their first night on the job.

The next day a couple of the guys bonded me out from the county jail. I had no defense in the Clarkins case, so I knew I needed a fix lawyer. I went to see Jerry Milano, a well-known defense attorney who enjoyed gambling. Jerry was arrogant but honorable. He knew a lot of people and could get things done, but it would cost an arm and leg. Criminals liked him because he was aggressive and outspoken during trials.

Jerry told me he couldn't help me with the parole violation, but he could get the Clarkins burglary time to run concurrent with the time I'd been sentenced for the California bank burglary. That sounded good to me. And so I went to court with Jerry and pled guilty to the Clarkins burglary.

Jerry was also able to delay the time between my guilty plea and the actual sentencing so that I could spend more time on the streets. It was six months after I pled guilty that I was in court for sentencing. And like Jerry had promised, the judge sentenced me for the Clarkins burglary but made my time for this state case concurrent with my time for the United California Bank federal case.

I paid Jerry a total of twenty-five thousand dollars in cash. As usual, so much of what I made in burglaries went toward attorney fees.

The Clarkins conviction immediately put me in violation of my federal parole. That didn't mean I'd immediately go to prison, though. I hadn't seen the U.S. marshals in court, but I knew they would be looking for me soon. It was just a matter of time until the paperwork for my state case reached the feds.

Two weeks later I had just pulled into the Society National Bank, which was one of the banks where I was trying to change six thousand dollars in hundreds to smaller bills. I had borrowed a friend's truck because I knew the U.S. Marshals would know my car. I'd just started to open the door of the truck when I noticed a car stop right behind me. Then one shot up in front of me, and then another. It was the marshals, and they had me. They had their guns out but didn't point them at me. They told me I was under arrest for parole violation, handcuffed me, and drove me downtown.

As we walked into Marshal's Office, one guy at a desk smiled and said, "You finally caught him."

Then one of the two marshals with me said, "And that isn't all. Can you believe he has about six thousand dollars on him?"

The other guy said, "What did you expect to find on him? That's Superthief."

Chapter Twenty-Eight

It was 1982, and once again I was back behind bars. A few months later, Diane divorced me. As usual, when I first got to a facility, there were a couple of guys waiting for me with a care package until I got settled in. The inmates gave me a toothbrush and toothpaste, other toiletries, and food from the commissary. All of the mob guys and anyone associated with them have a network. Word comes from the street about who is being sent where, and there are always a few guys to welcome him.

Tony Liberatore was one of them. He was with the Cleveland mob and had just been sent to prison for paying an FBI secretary to give him a list of informants. We got to be pretty good friends.

Tony introduced me to guy named Jimmy Burke who was from New York. The three of us were in the same unit, E-Block. Jimmy and I got to be friends because we knew a lot of the same guys from New York, Cleveland, and Chicago, and we would talk about scores we'd done. Jimmy told me the story of a young kid he'd taken under his wing. He became part of their crew but eventually ratted all of them out. His name was Henry Hill. He had a book written about him, and later it was made into a hit movie called Goodfellas, in which Robert

DeNiro played Jimmy.

While I was in prison, Jack Licavoli came through. Jack was eighty and had just been sentenced to seventeen years for federal racketeering charges in connection with the murder of Danny Greene. I felt bad when I saw him hobbling down the corridor with his cane. Jack was happy to see me, but he said he'd never make it out of prison alive. I tried to lift his spirits and tell him different, but I knew he was right.

One night in the winter of 1982, I called my friend Billy to see how the body shop was doing. Billy said he'd had to move to another spot because he wasn't doing that well. I wasn't all that upset about it. I only had about thirty thousand dollars in it.

Then Billy said, "Did you hear about the brothers?"

When he said brothers, the first thing that came to my mind was the Dinsio brothers, Amil and James.

"What about them?"

Billy seemed like he was beating around the bush. I couldn't imagine what he had to tell me about the Dinsios unless they'd got out on bond. Maybe they'd won their appeal. Billy had my curiosity up. But then he started to change the subject.

I said, "Wait, Billy, tell me about the Dinsio brothers."

"No, Phil, uh, it isn't the Dinsio brothers."

"Well, who is it?"

"You don't know about the article in the newspaper?"

Again Billy started playing cat and mouse with me.

Finally I said, "Billy, who in the fuck are you talking about?"

"Phil, remember that girl you use to go with a while back who had two brothers?"

Now I knew who he was talking about. The Kilbane brothers. Owen and Marty.

"So what about them?"

"They were indicted in an old murder. And, uh, your name was mentioned as the hit man."

I instantly got sick to my stomach, my heart started pounding, and my face felt flushed. I just sat there on the telephone in a daze, trying to think. I hung up the phone without saying goodbye. I went back to my cell, lay on my bunk, and stared at the ceiling. I'd always regretted that evening on Lake Erie fourteen years earlier. It was just before I started making big money as a burglar. I never imagined it would come back to haunt me, and I just knew it had to be Owen the pimp and his big mouth.

The following week I was called to the records office and told there were two men who wanted to see me. I didn't know the first guy, who was big with dark-rimmed glasses and short dark hair. The other one I recognized right away as a detective from the Cleveland Police. I knew this wasn't a social meeting. They didn't stick out their hands or stand up when I walked in the office.

The big guy said his name was Carmen Marino, and he introduced the detective. Carmen said he was from the Cuyahoga County Prosecutor's office. I had heard of him, and he had a very good reputation as a prosecutor. I sat down and listened to what else he had to say.

Carmen said, "You probably know by now what is going on."

"I heard about some article in the newspaper."

"First of all, I don't like your kind," Carmen said. "But if you want to come clean on the Arnie Prunella case, I will see what I can do for you."

"I don't have any lawyer with me. And until I have a lawyer to consult with, I don't have anything to say."

Carmen reached in his pocket and pulled out an envelope.

He said, "Is that it then?"

"That's it."

He handed me the envelope, and I got up and walked out of the office. Then I went back to my cell and opened the envelope. It was a True Bill from the Cuyahoga Grand Jury—an indictment for the murder of Andrew Prunella in 1968. I just took in a deep breath, shook my head, and sighed. I felt like I was in another world. All these years, and now they come down with an indictment.

About a month later I was waiting to get transported to Cleveland for the Arnie Prunella. I was talking with Tony Liberatore in his cell when the guard called my name out. Tony shook my hand and gave me a big hug. I saw a bunch of other Italian guys in my unit, who all knew I was going to court for a murder trial. I shook hands and got hugs and kisses on my cheek and wishes for good luck. I hated the hugs and kisses, but it made me feel good that I had friends who cared. I even saw a few guards I knew well, and they wished me good luck, too.

When I went downstairs to Receiving and Discharge, there were two detectives from Cleveland. They handcuffed me and put ankle cuffs on. Then they signed some papers and started leading me outside. As soon as I was walking up the ramp and going to the front gate, I heard a couple of guys I couldn't see yelling, "Go kick ass, Phil. We're in your corner."

I just kept walking until we got to the front tower and the guard opened the gate. It was a nice sunny day. We walked into the parking lot as I shuffled along with the ankle cuffs digging into my legs. I was thinking that the ride was going to be rough being shackled like this. Then the detectives stopped outside of these two unmarked police cars where another couple of detectives were waiting. As soon as they put me in the back seat, two of them opened one of the trunks, pulled out M-16 rifles, and brought them into the other car. I'd never seen detectives carry rifles to transport an inmate before, and I wondered what was going on.

My car took off from the prison, and the other followed right behind. After we were driving a few minutes, I said, "How come you have four guys, two cars, and the automatic weapons?"

"Phil, we're protecting you."

"Protecting me? From what?"

"Didn't anyone tell you? There is a rumor that Owen Kilbane put a contract out on you."

"You've got to be kidding."

I laughed to myself. I figured it had to be a ploy by the prosecutor's office. He'd probably tell me my life was in danger, and the only way out would be to testify against the Kilbanes. Over the years I'd learned that the law has a big bag of tricks to use against you.

The day after I got to Cleveland, my attorneys Chris Nardi and Mark DeVan came to see me. They didn't say anything about Owen putting a contract out on me, so I knew it was all bullshit. They said I'd be arraigned the next day and asked if I needed any money or cigarettes. I didn't smoke and I didn't need any money. Chris and Mark said they'd see me in court.

The next morning I was brought in front of Judge McMonagle. This was only a formality, and I entered a plea of not guilty. The Kilbane brothers had already been arraigned. I was taken away and locked up in a cell block called Protective Custody, where you weren't allowed to make any phone calls. I didn't know why they put me in there, but I figured they were still playing some kind of game to pit the Kilbane brothers and me against each other. I figured they were probably going to tell the Kilbane brothers that I was rolling over and going to testify against them. I was mad because I knew it was Owen's bragging that got us in trouble, but I wasn't going to roll over.

Chris Nardi and Mark DeVan told me they felt the case was weak. But I thought to myself it couldn't be too weak if I got indicted. Then they told me some of the names on the witness list. I didn't recognize any of them and figured they must have been some of the people Owen bragged to about killing Arnie Prunella.

I asked my attorneys to try and get me off the lock-up floor I was on, but it took several days before I was put on a regular floor and was able to make phone calls. I called my mother and father, and they said they'd see me at the courthouse.

On the morning of the trial, I was put in a holding cell. About ten minutes later, the guard unlocked the door and the Kilbane brothers were brought in. It had been eleven years since I'd seen them last. They had been serving time since 1977 for another murder, and both looked older. But they were the same characters—Owen the talker and Martin the quiet one. I shook hands with them but felt like punching Owen in his big mouth. He started right away when I saw him.

"Phil, we've been framed. They made this case up from nothing."

"Well, they must have something," I said. "They have a big list of witnesses. They seem to be all the people you know. I don't know any of them."

I asked Martin how he was doing. He said he had been going to school in prison and studying a lot.

Then Owen started again about us being framed. He just had to keep talking.

I said, "Look, Owen, let's just quit all this bullshit about being framed and work to beat this case."

The trial started off well for me. Carmen Marino was a good prosecutor but more or less bullied the jury. I felt good because it had been several days and I'd only heard Owen and Martin's names mentioned. Mark DeVan said I shouldn't even be there. My name hadn't been mentioned, and the State hadn't even proven there was a murder because no body was ever found. But the next day I got some bad news. Chris Nardi told me that Charles Broeckel, my old dear friend who'd turned rat eleven years ago, was going to testify that I told him I killed Arnie Prunella. I thought to myself, that lying mother-fucker. I never told him or anyone else about it. I never bragged to impress people.

Chris told me that Carmen Marino was willing to make a deal if I pled guilty. He said they'd reduce the charge to manslaughter and take me out of the murder trial. I didn't have to make a decision that day. I thought about it all night but still didn't know what to do.

The next day Chris Nardi told me he'd talked to Carmen Marino, who said that if I pled guilty to manslaughter, he'd try to get the time running concurrently with my federal sentence. I didn't give him an answer right away.

Chris went back to the courtroom, and I was put in a holding area with the Kilbanes. They were quiet when I came in.

Then Owen said, "What did your lawyer have to say?"

I said that Carmen Marino offered me a deal if I pled guilty. Owen asked what I was going to do. I told him I hadn't made a decision yet.

After the morning session, I asked Mark DeVan what he thought of the deal, but Mark said it was too soon to make deals. At the end of the day, Chris pulled me aside. He told me to think about the deal. I thought to myself, this shit is really getting frustrating. I have two attorneys, but it seems like they're not on the same page. It was really starting to wear on my nerves. I had lost a lot of weight, and my pants were a couple of sizes too big.

The next day court started as usual. There was a lot of testimony about people who'd heard Owen making references to killing Arnie. Of course, he denied it, but I know how pimps are. They're always trying to impress people.

There was another recess, and I was brought back to the holding cell. Chris Nardi again came back and got me, and this time he had Mark DeVan with him. Chris again said they wanted to offer me a deal. They left for about fifteen minutes, then Mark came back and wanted me to make up my mind. He said the judge was waiting in his chambers. My heart didn't want to plead guilty but my head thought it was the only choice or I wouldn't see the streets until I was an old man. And so I told Mark I was going to take the deal, provided I didn't have to testify against the Kilbanes.

Mark said, "Are you sure?"

I hated that he said that because I felt that maybe I was making the wrong decision. He knocked on the door, the guard opened it, and Mark told the guard to bring me into the judge's chambers. I was very nervous, and my heart was beating hard. A thousand thoughts were going through my head at once. What will my family think? Did I do the right thing? What will other people think?

Judge McMonagle was sitting behind his desk without his robe on. He stood up and shook my hand. I couldn't believe it. Why was the judge shaking my hand?

He said, "I believe you did the right thing. You will still be young enough when you get out of federal prison."

That made me feel like I'd made the right decision.

The judge chatted briefly and made me feel relaxed. Then he told his clerk to go and get Carmen Marino. A few minutes later, Carmen came in. Judge McMonagle said that whatever was discussed was put on a gag order. I didn't know what that meant, but when he asked me if I understood everything, I said I did but had one question.

"I understand that when I get done doing federal time, I won't have to go to state prison."

The judge said, "That is right."

"I also have another state sentence already running concurrently with the federal. So all these sentences will be running concurrently."

"That's right, everything will be together."

That sounded good to me. I wouldn't hurt the other guys going to trial. I just wouldn't be there anymore. The judge said he would instruct the jury to just forget about me being tried in that case. I felt relieved, like I was catching a break.

The judge sentenced me and told the deputy sheriffs who were in charge of me to send me back to prison as soon as possible. That was good news to my ears. I would be glad to go where I could get out and breathe some fresh air and see some sun. I shook hands with everybody, and the two sheriff's deputies took me downstairs. They said I'd made the right choice. That made me feel good.

I didn't see any of my family when I left the judge's chambers, but Mark said he would tell them. I felt like a ton of weight had just been lifted off my back. I could breathe again. By the time I got back to my cell, it was late, and there were a whole bunch of guys waiting to use the phone. I would have to call my family tomorrow. I just wanted to lie down.

I was awakened at 5:30 a.m.

The guard said, "Get your shit."

I said, "Where am I going?"

"You're leaving."

I couldn't believe it. I was glad that I was going, but I thought I would be around a few more days to see my family in the visiting room.

The deputy sheriffs came and got me in a big Lincoln. They said, "You're riding in style today."

I smiled. "Why a Lincoln?"

"County cars aren't insured outside the county, so we rent cars. There was a special on Lincolns this week."

We flew down the highway, and before I knew it, I was back in prison again. As crazy as it seemed, it felt good to be back. Tony Liberatore and my other friends in the joint were surprised but happy to see me. They had been keeping track by calling home every day to find out what was in the newspapers or on TV and radio. I told them what happened, and they said I'd made a good move.

Then Tony Lib and I sat in his cell, and I told him the whole story. I told him I felt like I had been beaten up. I went back to my single cell, which fortunately had been saved for me. I felt just totally worn out. I measured my pulse rate, and it was beating seventy-two beats per minute. My normal pulse was around sixty beats per minute. I went to sleep early because I was totally exhausted.

The next day I called home. My parents weren't home, and my brother wasn't home. Then I called Sandy to see how she was doing and what effect this trial had had on my son. She was glad to hear from me and said our son was doing okay. Then Sandy asked me if I'd heard they dismissed the case against the Kilbane brothers. I couldn't believe my ears. I felt like a real asshole—like I got used. I was very upset.

I told Sandy it was good talking to her, but I had to get in touch with my brother to find out what happened. I tried to call and call and couldn't get in touch with anybody. Then I told Tony what happened. He said to just relax and wait to find out what exactly happened. All I could think was if only I had waited one more day instead of pleading guilty, my case might have been dismissed, too.

That evening I finally got in touch with my brother. He told me that the judge declared a mistrial because my lawyer, Mark DeVan, got mad at a newspaper reporter who was making it sound like I was going to testify against the Kilbane brothers. So Mark broke the gag order the judge had imposed and told the newspaper what actually did happen in the judge's chambers. Then the judge fined Mark. My brother said he didn't believe the prosecution would re-indict the brothers. He felt I shouldn't have done what I'd done, but I thought, he doesn't have to do the time.

After I hung up, I called my parents. They were glad about what I'd done and that it was all over. I felt better that they were happy and pleased. So it really didn't matter to anybody who thought I was wrong.

Then I told Tony Lib what happened.

"Phil, you still made the right choice. You only have three more years to do."

That made me feel better.

It was time for me to get back into the swing of things and let this time go by. I would be out before I knew it.

A friend of mine who worked in Unicor, the prison industries, asked me if I wanted his job as a night-shift clerk. He was going to day shift. He showed me around the textile mill where they made blankets and towels. The machines sure were noisy, but it seemed like a pretty good gig. I would be in charge of about eighty guys and do all the paperwork and payroll for their overtime. So I started right away. I liked it because it was at night and away from the mainstream of guys in the evening when the most of them were in the unit making noise. Then when I got in at night, they were all locked down and asleep for the night. In the morning I could get up and work out, which I love to do, because mornings are when I'm my freshest and strongest.

After a little more than a month had gone by, I got a call to go to the records office, where two detectives introduced themselves to me. I had no idea what they wanted. And I didn't care.

I said, "I don't have anything to say. If you want to talk to me, see my lawyer first. I am not going to talk to anybody without my lawyer." Then I turned and walked out the door.

I heard one of them ask, "Don't you want to know why we're here?"

I just kept on walking till I got back to my unit. I thought to myself, you have to stand up to these people because if they think you're weak, they'll walk all over you.

A few hours later, I was called back down to records. The clerk said, "You sure got those detectives mad."

I just laughed.

He said, "They left this for you," and handed me an envelope.

I opened it and it was another murder indictment. For a Dr. Price back in 1969. I just shook my head and walked out the door and over to Tony Lib's cell.

I said, "You won't believe this, Tony. Do you remember me telling you about seeing those two agents yesterday? Guess what they left me. Never mind, because you probably couldn't guess."

I just handed the paper to him.

"Jesus Christ. Another one?" he said.

"That is what I said when I opened it. And it's all bullshit, Tony. It's nothing but a pressure tactic for me to rat out the Kilbane brothers on the Prunella case. I know about this murder. Charlie Broeckel shot Dr. Price during a burglary. I wasn't there, but I heard about it from the other guys Charlie was with."

I was very upset about all this but wasn't worried. It was nothing but a trick. It seems the more I dealt with the law and courts, the more I found out they were just full of tricks.

When I met with Mark DeVan, I found out that the main witness against me in the Dr. Price murder case was none other than my rat friend, Charlie Broeckel. I couldn't figure out why he would make up such a lie when he knew I wasn't even there. I knew I was innocent, but if Charlie lied on the stand, I could get convicted for a murder I didn't commit. And since this was a capital case, I could go to the chair over a bunch of lies.

After the first meeting with Mark and the other attorney, it was decided I would take a polygraph test. If I passed the test, Mark would request that the prosecutor give me and Charlie Broeckel polygraphs. At the time, the famous attorney F. Lee Bailey had a television program in which a polygraph expert would give tests, so we hired him. Needless to say, I passed with no problem. Mark was thrilled and took the results to Carmen Marino, the prosecutor, but he refused to give me a lie detector test, saying they couldn't be used in court anyway.

I was still trying to figure out why Charlie would testify that I shot Dr. Price when I wasn't there. My brother was doing a lot of legwork. He learned that Charlie had been kicked out of the witness protection program for committing a burglary and wanted back in because he couldn't make a living for himself. He was facing serious prison time, and Charlie had trouble doing thirty days. Then I heard he had been doing drugs and was also diagnosed with cancer. The guy must have been desperate. He made up lies so he could testify in court and get back in the witness protection program. As a result his whole family turned against him.

A few days before the trial, I happened to see Father Dismas, and I asked if I could talk to him. I discussed the case with him and told him I was worried about being convicted of a murder I did not commit. He said, "God be with you in the courtroom."

During the trial I had Charlie's ex-girlfriend and his own son as my witnesses. His girlfriend cried over how he mistreated her and lied about everything. Charlie's son testified about how his father got so angry one time that he actually shot at him. When he described the gun, my attorneys pointed out that the caliber and other characteristics matched the bullets recovered in the murder of Dr. Price.

Charlie's son was a very good kid who was nothing like his father. While he was testifying, he had a small black book in his hand, and after Carmen Marino was done questioning him, he asked him what the black book was. Charlie's son answered that it was a Bible and that he was a born-again Christian. I thought that sounded good to the jury. Carmen thanked him, sat down, and looked like he wanted to slide under the table.

During the trial Mark DeVan's mother passed away. He was a wreck and told me I should find someone else to represent me, but I told him I needed him. And so he was granted only one day off for his mother's funeral and continued to work with me. In his final argument, he made a very effective and passionate presentation that was like a scene out of a movie. He noted that Charlie should have come forward with his knowledge of the Price murder when he was debriefed during the investigation involving the police lookouts. Charlie's holding back that information and bringing it up now, after he was kicked out of the witness protection program, was very damaging to his credibility. Mark flat-out accused him of lying about his role in the murder of Dr. Price, pointed out numerous discrepancies in Charlie's testimony, and painted him as a cunning, pill-popping liar and vicious killer.

In the end I was acquitted in the Dr. Price murder trial. Charlie was never even charged.

After fighting two murder indictments, going back to Terre Haute was like being on vacation. I would be in prison for two-and-a-half more years.

Chapter Twenty-Nine

It was late in the fall of 1986 when I was sitting in the Receiving and Discharge room waiting to be paroled.

I heard one guard ask the other, "What is that big black limo doing outside?"

The other one answered, "That's for Christopher."

"Oh, that's right. He's one of those Mafia guys."

The guard opened the heavy iron door, and I walked out and jumped into the limo with my brother and couple of friends. I didn't look back as we drove off. My brother asked where I wanted to go, and I said I wanted a drink. We stopped at a restaurant about ten miles down the road and had couple of beers.

When I got home, it was party time for two weeks. After that I got permission from my parole officer to see my parents, who were vacationing in Florida for the winter. I stayed two days with my mother and father in Fort Lauderdale, and I looked up several friends from Cleveland who had moved to Florida. It was like old times as we partied all over Florida. In the daytime we relaxed in the sun by the pool, and at night we hit the strip clubs. I never knew there were so many strip joints in Florida. Some stayed open until 5:00 a.m. I only had a week before I had to be home and report back to my parole officer.

And so I snuck over to Georgia and spent several days with some girl I met before I went away.

When I got back home, I had to rest from all the partying. Then I called Howard Blum, a guy from Youngstown who had served some time with me in prison. Howard would sometimes talk too much and piss off some of the inmates, and I'd have to step in to keep him from getting hurt. That's how we got to be good friends.

Howard was living in Youngstown and told me to come down. He threw a big party for me and gave me a 1981 Mercury, five thousand dollars cash, and some cocaine to sell. In no time I had most of my old customers back and was in the drug business again.

Then I met this girl named Anna, who was a barmaid at a sports bar where I was hanging out. We started dating and in May of 1987 we got married.

Looking back, this period of my life seems like a blur. I was moving fast and trying to play catch-up for all the years I was in prison. I was selling cocaine and making money like I had a printing machine. And I was spending it, too. I bought a two-family house in Collinwood where I could be close to my parents. Anna and I moved into the lower unit and rented out the upper one. She'd always wanted a horse, so I bought her an Arabian that she boarded in a rural area just outside the city. I also got us a champion bloodline German Shepherd.

I wanted to take care of my son, too, since I didn't have the chance to see him grow up and spend time with him. He was then twenty years old. I bought him a landscaping company from some guy he used to work for, a pick-up truck, and a new dump truck with a snowplow. I also got his mother's car fixed up at a body shop and bought her a big wall-to-wall rug for her house, which is where my son was living.

After I took care of my family, I spent a few dollars on myself. I bought a limited edition, candy-apple-red Harley. I hopped from bar to bar on my new toy and spent a lot of time at this strip joint called the Executive Den. While Anna was busy playing with her Arabian horse, I was playing around with several girls. Then I met Kelly, who was a stripper at the Executive Den. We got to be pretty close, and I wound up setting her up in an apartment on the East Side. I was having a great time.

In 1989, I started noticing undercover cops watching me. They would follow me on my Harley, double-teaming me with two different unmarked cars. They would park at both ends of my street to make sure they caught me leaving the house. One time I was jogging in my neighborhood when I saw them criss-crossing the streets following me. I had some fun with them by jumping over fences and going from street to street. Then I bought another car and parked it on the street behind my house. I could jump the fence behind my house and get to the car without them seeing me.

I assumed my phone was tapped, so whenever I needed to make a call, I got my linemen's handset and tapped into the line for the renter that lived upstairs. And since I knew the law might search my house someday, I never kept drugs there. One day when Kelly wasn't home, I built a hiding place under the floor of her storage unit, which was down the hall from her apartment. I copied her key and would keep my stash there. I was always trying to stay one or two steps ahead of the law.

But in the world of crime, staying one step ahead of the law can be extremely difficult, especially when you can't even trust your best friend. I'd learned that with Charlie Broeckel, but this time it was Howard Blum. While we were making an exchange of a kilo of cocaine, he was wired. He had been indicted for drugs, but he cut a deal to set me up.

I was being held in the Euclid City Jail on the east side of Cleveland and trying to make the best of it. One Saturday night I knew the captain of the jail was on vacation. I told the guard supervisor that if he got someone to go and get pizzas for everyone in the jail, then I'd buy. At first he didn't want to do it, but I convinced him that all the prisoners would be happy and nobody would find out. I paid for a dozen or so large pizzas that night. All the prisoners and guards ate them, and we had a great time.

But then the following week, the captain returned. Someone told him what we had done, and the supervisor and I got in trouble. The captain was screaming at me, "Who the hell do you think you are having a pizza pie party in my jail?"

Also while I was in that jail, Mark DeVan told me that a writer from Cleveland Magazine wanted to do a story on me. But for some reason, the guy never showed up. Mark told me I should write a book about my life because of all the wild and unusual things I had done.

When my case came up in court, I took a plea deal for twelve years. I got hit hard because of my past record. It was 1991, and I was once again behind bars, this time at Milan, Michigan, a medium-security prison where Joseph Valachi was kept when he was testifying against the mob during the fifties. Milan was laid back compared to Terre Haute, which is maximum security. Except for the fences, razor wire, and guard towers, it looked like a college campus. Milan was about as old as Terre Haute, but the three-story buildings spread around looked fairly new.

The inside compound at Milan was one big square encircled by dormitories, the hole, the lieutenants' and captains' offices, the chow hall, the commissary, and Unicor, the prison industry program. This was the original Milan until they built the two new buildings and later a third one.

There were about eight hundred guys in Milan. The cells were like college dorm rooms. There was one guy to a big room with a bed, toilet, sink, and a desk and chair. You even had your own key to your room. There were three tiers of these cells and four TV rooms. It was sweet.

The food in the Milan chow hall was good, and their bakery department put out some great pastry. During the summers at Milan, they even had barbecues. We also had a lot of fresh vegetables from the garden program. There were one hundred three-by-ten-foot garden plots raffled off in April. The recreation department would give us a few tomato plants, hot pepper plants, and various seeds, and then we'd take care of our own gardens.

My time in Milan was also when I first started working on my life story. This time it was Howard Siegrist, another attorney, who suggested it. We were on the phone discussing my case when he brought it up. I thought about it and decided to go for it. And so I began with an outline of important events, then started writing about my life from when I was a little boy. As I continued writing, I eventually got copies of some of the more than 35,000 pages the FBI had in my file at the time.

In Milan I also had a few different jobs. My first was supervisor of the grounds crew. There were about seventy inmates who cut the grass, plowed snow, and did clean-up. Around 1993, I left the grounds crew and worked in Unicor, where we made lockers and storage racks that were used by federal agencies. I did quality assurance work on the paint jobs, but since my lungs were already weakened from having TB, I got a lot of bronchial infections from breathing paint fumes and dust. As a result I left Unicor and worked my last years at Milan in the commissary where I filled inmate orders. When I wasn't at work, I spent much of my time lifting weights, jogging, and working on my life story.

Chapter Thirty

In the fall of 1997, my father was in the hospital and very sick. During the first few weeks of September I was calling him almost every day to tell him I loved him. On September 21, I was called to the chaplain's office. I knew what it was for. The chaplain dialed my mother, and we both cried on the phone.

I had already made arrangements with my case manager to attend my father's funeral. For an inmate to attend a funeral, he had to have a minimum of one thousand dollars deposited in his prison account to pay for a guard escort and related expenses. I had the money, and my case manager had completed all the necessary requirements.

Later that day my case manager told me there was a problem with the paperwork she put through, and the warden wasn't going to let me go. When I spoke to the warden about it, he said that this was the first he'd heard of it, he never got any paperwork, and he'd look into it. I called my mother and asked if she could push things back a couple of days. That would give me enough time to get the problem straightened out.

Two days later my case manager said everything was set. The funeral was the next day, and two corrections officers were going to take me. We'd be leaving at 6:00 a.m. That would give us plenty of time to get to DiCicco's Funeral Home in Mayfield Heights, on the east side of Cleveland, by 10:00 a.m. I would be paying for the costs of the guards beyond their scheduled eight-hour shift. I also had to pay for gas.

The next morning I was dressed in my uniform and ready to leave. Six o'clock came and went. At 7:00 a.m., I was trying to get in touch with my case manager, but she hadn't come in yet. I was so angry I could chew nails. I was trying to get the lieutenant of the guards to do something, but he said it was out of his hands. Even my friends were complaining to him. Finally 8:00 a.m. came and went. Now I was beyond angry—I was just totally depressed. There was no way I could make it to Cleveland by 10:00 a.m. It was a three-and-a-half hour drive.

When I called my mother and told her I wouldn't be able to make it, she started crying. It tore me up inside. I hung up and could have killed someone, but I just went to my cell to be alone. I started to take my clothes off when one of the guards told me to go to Receiving and Discharge. I knew what that meant. They'd finally got the okay to take me, but it was too late.

I went down to R&D, where there were two guards who were well-dressed in sport coats. I told them it was too late—I'd missed my father's funeral. I knew these two guys well and they said they were going to try, but I told them there was no way we'd make it.

One of them said, "Phil, you're wasting time. Let's go. We'll get you there."

They handcuffed me, and as we quickly walked out to the car, they explained that the captain's office had forgotten to schedule my guard escort. I just shook my head in disgust. It was a good thing I'd talked to the warden. After we got outside, the guards put leg shackles on me. I got in the back of the white Crown Victoria, and we shot out of the parking lot.

The driver was hitting one hundred miles per hour on the freeway while the other one was watching out for traffic. I thought to myself, these guys are serious. It made me feel good that they were trying so hard.

When we got close to Cleveland, they asked me which exit they should take. I looked at the clock on the dashboard and thought for a second, then told them to go right to Lakeview Cemetery where my father was being buried, since nobody would be at the funeral home. They asked me again what exit. It was a long time since I had driven in Cleveland, and I couldn't think of how to get to the cemetery. We were passing downtown Cleveland, and I told them to get off at Martin Luther King Road. We were off the freeway now, and I was praying that I'd told them the right way.

We got to Euclid Avenue, and I knew I'd guessed right. Then we passed by Little Italy and pulled into Lakeview, which was a very big cemetery. The one guard got out and went into the office to find out where to go. He came back fast and told the driver which way to go. We turned a couple of times and went about a half mile, then I could see people and a bunch of cars ahead. The driver was going about thirty miles per hour—pretty fast for a cemetery. I started recognizing faces of my family now. The driver came to an abrupt stop near the gathering, and everyone was looking. I could see from everyone's faces that they didn't know who it was.

The driver got out first and went around to the passenger side. Then the other guard got out. I could see all of the crowd standing there and just mesmerized by this white car that had pulled up. The guards opened my door and helped me get out. The one officer asked me what cuffs I wanted off because they were required to leave one restraint on. I said the handcuffs because this way I could hold people. So they left the ankle cuffs on.

As we got closer to the grave, all of my cousins came running up to me. I could see the rest of my family, the Christophers, all crying. I was trying to smile and was able to until I got by the casket, where my mother and my son were. I was still holding up strong. The funeral director, a good friend from childhood, hugged me and cried. Then he asked me if I wanted to see my father. I told him I would really appreciate it, and so he unlocked the casket. That was all it took. I broke down crying. I had been calling my father every day for the last couple of weeks that he was alive just to tell him I loved him. Now I touched my father, kissed him, and for the last time told him that I loved him.

My cousins talked to the correctional officers and invited them back to the funeral home where there would be a gathering and food. While I was at the tables with my mother and the rest of my family, the officers stayed in a separate room and ate and smoked. At one point I talked to my mother alone and told her that when I got out of prison, it would be just the two of us.

We were at the funeral home at least three hours. On the way back to Milan, the officers said I had a wonderful family. They had eaten so much food they couldn't move. I could see they had been very relaxed around me and my family.

Chapter Thirty-One

In 1998, I was released from Milan. It had been my longest stretch of time served, and things had sure changed on the streets. Many of Collinwood's white residents had moved east into the suburbs as more black families continued to move into the area. My mother had bought a house in Mayfield Heights where a lot of Italians lived. I moved in with her.

Driving was a new experience. Traffic everywhere was heavier, and there were freshly built express lanes on the freeway. The first time I went to get gas in my brother's car, I couldn't figure out how to work the pump. When I asked another driver for help, he looked at me like I was retarded. In downtown Cleveland, the Rock and Roll Hall of Fame had gone up, and the old Cleveland stadium had been replaced by Jacob's Field. And I had heard of cell phones, but it seemed that everyone was carrying a miniature one.

I tried to get a job in the labor unions where I knew a lot of the bosses. But the federal government was overseeing the hiring and assigning of jobs because there had been so much corruption when organized crime was in control. My friends apologized over and over as they turned me down for jobs, but they said I'd draw too much attention from the feds. I told them I understood and didn't want to cause them any problems. But deep down I felt they were wrong and didn't have any balls.

Still hoping to retire from crime permanently, I started looking into rehabbing real estate—buying property, fixing it up, and reselling it for a profit. My brother set up an appointment with a real estate company, and we were sitting in TGI Friday's restaurant waiting for them. Two of them came in—a man and woman. The woman was sharp and I figured her to be about twenty-eight, a little young for me. But it had been a long time in prison and I have to admit, when I saw Mary Ann, I no longer had real estate on my mind. We exchanged greetings, and she wound up sitting next to me. She didn't have a wedding ring.

We started talking about the real estate business, and she seemed so well-educated and professional. Her face and hands looked so soft and delicate, and her blonde hair was styled nicely. I sure liked what I saw.

The table was small. We were bunched together, and every now and then my leg accidentally bumped Mary Ann's leg. Then sometimes it would purposely bump her leg. I was looking at her out of the corner of my eye but not getting any response. I was trying not to stare but did keep glancing at her. I thought to myself, I'll have to start practicing up on my charm.

MARY ANN: When we walked into TGI Friday's, Philip and his brother were already there seated at a table. His brother waved to me, but all I saw was Philip. I was immediately attracted to him and became nervous. We all shook hands and sat down. Philip sat next to me—rather close. We started talking business, but Philip was quiet. He was taking everything in. After a while his leg bumped mine. I moved over a little. A minute later so did he.

Over the next few days, Philip came to my office, and I took him out to see properties. He started taking me to lunch and calling me every morning. I loved it, but I was nervous. I was a divorced mother of two girls, and I knew he was— how should I put it—a worldly man.

PHIL: Here I was back in the free world, being driven around by a classy-looking blonde and having the sun shining down on us through her sun-roof. I would hang around Mary Ann's office, and she'd show me how the computers worked. After she got off, we'd go out to dinner. They were beautiful days. I felt like James Cagney in The Public Enemy: "Look, Ma! I'm on top of the world!"

One afternoon she invited me out to her house, her hideout as I called it because it was across town from where her family lived. We were supposed to go over some real estate contracts, but that's not what I was interested in. I didn't get what I was after, but it turned out to be a good night. Her lips against mine felt fantastic, and I even got a back rub.

Things progressed with Mary Ann, but the rehab business didn't pan out for me. We just couldn't find the right houses that would give me a profit.

I wanted to live with Mary Ann, but I was living with my mother and didn't want to hurt her. She was eighty years old and I knew she had been very lonely since my father died. I know what an awful feeling loneliness is, and I had promised I'd live with her when I got out of prison. I loved my mother and I loved Mary Ann—I was torn between two people whose feelings I didn't want to hurt. But I knew I would have to tell my mother I'd be moving out. It was one of the hardest things I ever did.

MARY ANN: One night at dinner, Philip got a serious look on his face.

"I need to let you know something," he said.

"What is it?"

"I've been institutionalized. I'm sorry."

"I know, Philip," I said. "I told you I've known your father since I was a kid. You don't have to apologize. You paid your debt to society. It's wonderful. You have a new beginning to your life."

I looked in this man's eyes and all I saw was sorrow. I could feel his sorrow in my heart.

In October 1999, Philip proposed to me. We planned to marry in September, 2000. In the meantime I left the real estate business because I didn't like pressuring people to buy a house. I'd always wanted my own business, so I opened a boutique. Philip helped me around the shop, and I couldn't have been happier. We were also looking into opening a deli.

I was keeping an eye on Philip as best I could without angering him. And he was still living with his mother. Every morning he'd call me 6:30, then pick me up for work. Things were going so well, and then some guys bought a vacant seafood store across the street from my shop. The odds had to be a million-to-one, but it turned out they were organized crime figures whom Philip knew very well. I could have just died when I would look over and see him standing on the sidewalk and talking to them. One day we got into a big argument about it. I called him on the cell phone.

I said, "Philip can you come over here please."

"I'll be over in a minute."

"No, I mean right now."

He came over and asked what was wrong, and I said, "Philip, do you know what it looks like with you talking to those guys? Look at them over there. Do you have any idea how that looks?"

He said, "It's okay, baby. Don't worry about it."

"I am worried about it. I'm worried about you."

Then on June 14, Philip was late picking me up. He was never late. And he didn't call. He always called. I had a bad feeling inside. I tried his cell phone, and there was no answer.

Chapter Thirty-Two

PHIL: All I wanted to do was get into a good business and make a decent living. I wasn't looking to be a millionaire anymore. I just wanted to lie back and enjoy life, but I needed financing to open the deli. I knew I could never qualify for a legitimate business loan, so I got involved with some guys who could help me. It was a huge mistake because they were moving marijuana and cocaine in a multi-state operation.

At 5:45 a.m. on June 14, 2000, I was startled awake by loud banging on the front door, which set off the burglar alarm in my mother's house. The pounding on the front door sounded all too familiar. My heart started racing.

I walked to the front and peeked out the window between the shades. There was a line of cars and vans parked in the driveway, and I could see about eight guys standing on the porch. They banged on the door a second time.

I went to the front door, and through the window I saw this one FBI agent who had arrested me in 1989. I yelled that I had to turn the alarm off, but they kept yelling for me to open the door. I knew it was senseless to run because they had the house surrounded. And so I walked to the rear of the house and turned the alarm off. There were more agents in the backyard and a car in the back driveway. My mother was yelling from her bedroom, calling for me and asking what was happening. I couldn't tell her it was the FBI coming for me.

As I walked slowly to the front door, so many things were going through my mind: my life history of crime, jails, courts, prisons, family, friends, and Mary Ann. I unlocked the front door and the agents quickly poured in, guns drawn. They spoke loudly that I was under arrest—as if I didn't know. They cuffed my hands behind my back. Then my mother came out of her bedroom and asked what was going on. An agent told her I was under arrest for drug charges, and she started crying and sobbing.

"He couldn't do that!" she screamed. "He's been so good."

I couldn't believe what was happening. My mother was crying so hard it broke my heart. As I was led to a van, all I could think was that Mary Ann would go through the roof when she found out. And I knew it wouldn't be too long because I was supposed to call her that morning like always did. I got a sick feeling inside that I wouldn't be with her for many years. Or maybe never again.

The weather was so beautiful that morning. It was warm and the sun was shining. But in my heart there was darkness. I was very lonely and just wanted to hold Mary Ann. I used to tell her she was my sunshine and I needed her beside me. Every morning when I picked her up, just the sound of her voice would bring a smile to my face. No matter how low I was, she always managed to lift my spirits. She was so sweet and beautiful. Her mind was so sharp and quick. I used to sit back in amazement at the words she would speak when dealing with lawyers and people in general.

As we traveled to the federal courthouse, I knew I was in serious trouble because of my past record. I felt like my life was over and what I'd always feared was coming true—that I would die in prison. I'd never felt that depressed in my life. I just wanted to stop breathing.

MARY ANN: I called Philip's house and his brother told me that Philip had been arrested. I didn't believe him. I asked what for, and he said drugs. I felt like the wind had been knocked out of me. He said there was a big raid, and they'd brought a drug-sniffing dog through the house. Twenty-eight people had been picked up in Ohio and California.

I had to tell his son and was thinking to myself, oh my God, what can I say to him. But I didn't want him to find out from strangers. I called him and told him I had to see him before he left for work. When I got to his house, I could see in his face that he knew something was wrong. When I told him his father had been arrested for drug trafficking, he was very disappointed. He asked if the allegations were true. I told him I didn't believe they were.

Two days later I visited Phil in jail. I spoke to him through thick glass using a telephone. He was shaking his head slowly.

"This is bad. This is real bad," he said.

I was crying hard.

"Phil, is it true what they're saying?"

He kept shaking his head and wiping tears from his eyes.

I said, "I thought you loved me."

"I'm sorry, Mary Ann. Please forgive me."

PHIL: All my life I'd been an honorable person, never willing to give up my friends to get out of prison time. That was the way of the old-time criminal. But over the years things had changed dramatically. There was no more honor and respect among criminals. It was out of control, and friends were ratting on friends left and right. People would tell me I was living in the past.

As I saw each co-defendant in the case, many said to me, "What are you doing here? They don't have anything on you." But there I was, right in the middle of a hornet's nest.

Facing career criminal charges, I figured I would die in prison. I was in a state of numbness, with my mind just going from one thing to another, playing my whole life history over and over again. And there was no escaping. I was trapped. During the next two weeks, some of the other defendants were bickering back and forth about what evidence the FBI might have against them. All I had to do was listen, and I could tell who was going to talk in exchange for a good deal. It wasn't like the old days when everyone kept their mouths shut.

Then one of the guys received a letter and made the mistake of opening it in front of one of the other co-defendants. The letter said that he was scheduled to meet with the U.S. attorney, an FBI agent, and his own lawyer. It was apparent that he was rolling over. I knew this guy was a weak person who would lie about my involvement if it meant saving himself. And because of my criminal history, I knew that the young FBI agents would consider me a trophy if they got a conviction.

When I heard this, I got a message to a good friend of mine who had also been arrested in the case. I told him to save himself by taking a plea deal. I knew he was going to get rolled over on, and to fight it in a trial, he'd wind up getting thirty years.

About a month after the arrest, I was transferred to a jail just outside of Cleveland and put in a cell with another guy. He told me about a series of books called Left Behind. They were taken from the Book of Revelations and made into a story. I was at the lowest I had ever been, and I needed help. And so I got involved in the religious program they had there. I prayed and prayed, asking forgiveness and seeking help from God. I prayed for Mary Ann and her daughters, for my mother, my brother, my son, and my grandchildren.

When my case came up, I decided to take a plea deal. If I went to trial and someone lied, I would easily be convicted and sent away for life. My attorney, Richard Drucker, worked out a pretty good plea bargain for me. I was going to get ten years. It was a long time, but at least I wouldn't die in prison.

MARY ANN: I was in court when Philip was sentenced on November 11, 2000. I was aware that he had accepted a plea deal. He was getting sentenced to ten years for drug conspiracy, and I was trying not to panic. We can do this, I thought to myself. There would be time off for good behavior, and I was doing the math in my head. He'd be out in eight-and-a-half years. The judge read Phil's sentence, I looked at him and whispered, "I love you," and he was led away.

Philip and I made plans to be married in the county jail in Cleveland on June

14, 2001, exactly one year after his arrest. I didn't want it to be my anniversary, but it was the only day the reverend could arrange to marry us.

My mother and daughters tried to make it a special occasion. They got a floral bouquet for me and a boutonniere for Philip and ordered a little cake. It was an awkward day. I left work at 11:00 a.m. and drove downtown to the Justice Center. I was wearing a pair of gray linen slacks and a matching gray summer sweater. The guards let me in, and I had to wait a half hour until they were ready. The prison pastor came in and talked to me about the seriousness of what I was doing. He wanted me to understand how difficult it would be. But I told him he didn't understand how difficult it would be for me to live without Philip. He wished me luck and said he would pray for God to keep me strong.

My own priest came in, and we were all escorted up to a room used for attorney visits. A few minutes later, Phil was escorted in. He wasn't allowed to wear anything special, so he just had on the jail's blazing orange jumpsuit. Our pastor began the service by talking about our commitment to each other. He said it wasn't going to be an easy road under the circumstances. He gave a beautiful sermon about the significance of a wedding ring, a perfect circle that was unending like our love for each other should be. I cried through the whole ceremony and could barely say "I do" because of the lump in my throat. Phil was thrilled that we were finally married, but he was sad for me having a jailhouse wedding. We got to kiss each other after the ceremony and have a forty-five minute visit. The two guards had to stay in the room, but they tried their best to give us some space. Phil kept telling me to stop crying. He was smiling and offering encouragement as he put his hands on my face and called me Mrs. Christopher.

"It'll be all right, honey," he told me. "Before you know it, this nightmare will be over."

When the guards called time, Phil and I kissed one more time and said goodbye. Then I went back to work. The girls there had cards for me and kept asking me if I was okay. After work my mother and daughters had a little celebration for me at home. My mother made a little cake, and my daughters bought me a bottle of champagne, which I'm saving for when Philip comes home. Later he called on the phone, and I told him about the cake and champagne. Then my daughters got on the phone and said, "Congratulations, Stepdad." Philip said he would call me the next day.

I had been married twice before, and one of my husbands died. But being apart from Philip is worse, because there is no finality of the grieving. It's like he dies every day. You know he's somewhere, but you can't touch him. I write to him frequently, and he calls me every other day. I picture him in my mind often and can sometimes even feel him. I say goodnight to him every night and don't sleep on his side of the bed.

In August 2001, Phil was shipped out of Cleveland. After several weeks on the road, he was sent to the federal prison at Allenwood, Pennsylvania. The visits are very hard. I have to arrange to take off work, drive six hours to Pennsylvania, have my visit, then drive back all in one day so I can be back to work the next morning. And the visits are very emotional. Of course, the most difficult part is saying goodbye, knowing that I won't see him for at least another month.

In 2003, Phil was moved from Allenwood to Loretto, Pennsylvania because his security level dropped from medium to low. This was a good thing because Loretto is closer to Cleveland than Allenwood is.

I just wait for the day that I can bring him home. I want us to feel the sun on our faces. I want to watch him sleep safe and sound and hear him breathe. People ask me, "Why did you marry him?" They ask, "How can you live like that?"

It's because I love him. He is part of me, and if I just quit and tried to go on with my life, I would still love him. He is my husband, my lover, and most important, my friend. I will always be here for him. And God forbid if something happens to him, I want to be able to take care of him.

Chapter Thirty-Three

In March 2003, a fellow inmate at Loretto told Phil that his name was in a book called *Justice Is Served*, which was co-authored by a well-known FBI agent named Robert Ressler. Phil read the book, which was mainly about the Marlene Steele murder case. Back in 1977, Owen and Martin Kilbane had been convicted of assisting Robert Steele, a municipal judge, in killing his wife. It was one of Ohio's most notorious murder cases. Steele died while incarcerated, and in recent years, the Kilbane brothers had been gaining ground in their battle to get paroled.

According to the book, during the late 1980s, Owen Kilbane wrote to and called Agent Ressler. He wanted the agent to visit him in person to "clear the air." Ressler told Owen that he would not see him unless he was more specific about what he had to offer. In 1989, Owen told Ressler he was ready to talk openly about the Steele and Prunella cases. In exchange Owen wanted help getting paroled. Later that year Ressler and another agent visited Owen and Martin twice and tape-recorded the interviews.

PHIL: From reading *Justice Is Served* it was apparent that before he even contacted Robert Ressler, Owen had talked about the Prunella case to several other people, including his wife and Robert Steele. Now I knew for sure that his mouth never stopped. And now I knew for sure that I'd done the right thing back in 1983 when I was offered the opportunity to plead guilty to a lesser charge than first degree murder and didn't have to testify against the Kilbane brothers. If I hadn't I'm sure Owen Kilbane would have rolled over on me to save himself.

Shortly after I read *Justice Is Served*, a number of newspaper articles in the Cleveland Plain Dealer reported that Cuyahoga County Prosecutor Bill Mason was trying to stop the Kilbanes from getting paroled. I had a feeling I'd be hearing from the prosecutor's office soon. They would want to use me as a pawn.

Sure enough, in August 2003, I was subpoenaed in front of the Cuyahoga County Grand Jury, which was investigating the Kilbane brothers' involvement in the murder of Arnie Prunella. Prosecutors had discovered new evidence in the 1968 murder and sought indictments against the Kilbanes.

I talked to my attorney about whether or not I should appear before the grand jury. I asked him what might be in it for me, but he said the assistant prosecutor was non-committal. The other side of the coin was what might happen if I didn't answer their questions.

While held in Cleveland for the grand jury proceedings, I went to mass. The next morning I went to confession and told Father Dismas the whole story of that evening in 1968.

It all started like this. Owen Kilbane told me he was being threatened by another pimp named Arnie Prunella. Though they had been allies, Owen thought the guy was going to kill him over some gambling conflict. I was dating Owen's sister, and she begged me to help. Owen Kilbane wanted to pay someone to have Arnie murdered, and he kept bugging me to find someone to do it. Finally I decided to do it myself. Owen gave me a thousand dollars up front, and I was supposed to get more later.

One night we lured Arnie on a boat and got him out onto Lake Erie. I was driving the boat and told Arnie, look at that bunch of stars to our left. When Arnie looked up, I shot him in the back of the head. He just collapsed onto the floor of the boat and was dead instantly. He never knew what hit him. And I never thought that night would come back to haunt me.

My confession took about thirty minutes. Father Dismas made me feel comfortable and gave me my penance. I thanked him, returned to my cell, and started praying.

While I waited in Cuyahoga County Jail for several days, my mind was racing about what the grand jury might ask me. I wasn't sure what to do. I certainly had no sense of allegiance to the Kilbane brothers. After all, it was Owen's bragging about killing Arnie Prunella that got us indicted in the first place.

On the morning of the grand jury session, the bailiff came and told me and my attorney, Richard Drucker, that they were ready for me. I told Richard I really wanted to take the Fifth Amendment and not answer any questions. But I was concerned that I'd get charged with contempt of court or that the prosecutor might come after me on other unsolved cases that they had information on. After we talked for a couple of minutes, Richard said he thought it would be best if I cooperated. The bailiff came back and was sort of cocky. He said the grand jury was waiting. I told him I still wasn't ready but had to bite my tongue from saying what I really wanted to say.

Then the assistant prosecutor came out to talk to me. I was still trying to see if there might be something in it for me, but the guy was being a real prick.

He said, "Look, I'm not doing anything for you. If you don't want to cooperate with the grand jury, then you don't have to. But I'm not making any deals with you. Now the grand jury is waiting, so you're going to have to make up your mind."

After another couple of minutes of weighing the pros and cons, I decided to answer the questions.

After I testified before the grand jury, I found out that the prosecutor wasn't happy with my testimony. Apparently he was frustrated that my recall of details about the Prunella murder was not stronger. The case was only thirty-five years old.

As punishment I was sent back to Loretto with maximum restraints. My hands were handcuffed then secured with a steel anti-escape box that dug into my wrists and stopped the blood circulation in my hands for sixteen hours.

Several months later, in April 2004, a friend of the Kilbanes who was also an acquaintance of mine got a message to me. "Owen wants you to help him find the people who saw Arnie Prunella in 1972."

I couldn't believe it. They were trying to intimidate me. I was so mad I could've chewed them up and spit them out. Did they really think they could pull off some phony witness saying that Prunella was still alive? Apparently the guy who sent the message never read *Justice Is Served*. If Arnie Prunella was alive, then what was Owen doing running his mouth off to the author about Arnie's murder?

During this time I found out more about the case against the Kilbanes. For years Owen's common-law wife had refused to testify against him, but she was a born-again Christian who felt that Owen could not have a genuine relationship with his sons until he accepted responsibility for the Prunella murder. She had information about the murder directly from Owen and was now willing to talk. And so with her testimony, coupled with other witnesses and dragging me back to court, Cuyahoga County Prosecutor Bill Mason would have the Kilbanes backed into a corner. They would be offered an attractive plea deal, and there'd be no trial. That was my prediction because I knew how the system works. The vast majority of criminals cases are settled by plea bargain. Very few actually go to trial.

In August 2004, a year after my grand jury testimony, I was returned to Cleveland for the scheduled trial. It was nice to be home because I thought I'd be able to see Mary Ann often. But I was housed at a suburban jail that only allowed one visit per week. Then just before the trial was to start, the Kilbanes were offered a deal like I thought they'd be. They pled out, and Owen got five years and Martin three. A few days later, I was back at Loretto. I sure was glad that chapter in my life was finally over.

Epilogue

As one retired police chief put it, "If there was a burglary Hall of Fame, it was in Cleveland's Collinwood neighborhood during the sixties and seventies." Phil Christopher certainly earned his place in that particular Hall of Fame. The 1972 burglary of the United California Bank remains the biggest in U.S. history, with a haul estimated at $30 million gross.

Nowadays bank burglaries are a rare crime. With advances in security technology and law enforcement, few thieves penetrate beyond the lobby. In fact, ATM machines located outside the bank are a much more likely target than the bank building itself.

Although Phil Christopher's place in crime history is therefore likely to remain secure, for him it is small compensation for having spent thirty-two of his sixty-one years behind bars.

PHIL: They say crime doesn't pay. It does pay, but just not for long. It's a rotten investment that will eventually suck the life out of you. When I get out of prison, I'll be sixty-five. Worst of all, I've broken Mary Ann's heart and squandered away the best part of my son's youth. I was never there for the birthdays,

Little League games, and bedtime stories. I wasn't there when my son got married and had children of his own. I couldn't be there when my father was sick
and dying. I pray that God keeps my mother around so I can spend time with
her when I'm released.

Some people have to hit bottom, then with the grace of God they find a better path. God showed me that better path. And I have faith that He will give me
the strength to stay on that road. My plans are to live lawfully and in peace. I
want to spoil Mary Ann as best I can and enjoy watching our grandchildren
grow. That sounds good to me.

• • •

Recently moved to the federal correction camp at Elkton, Ohio, Phil is ten-
tatively scheduled to be released in 2009.

Visit
Superthief.com

About the Author

Tonight is a mixed-emotion night for a lot of us in my family, ladies and gentleman. We're losing a member of the family. He's gonna get out of the business and pursue another career and it's our loss, not only on a personal basis, but I think it's music's loss, too. I want to wish him publicly what I said to him privately: May God put his arms around him and may he be as successful doing his new job as he has been for the two-and-a-half years that we've had the pleasure of his company. He's contributed so much and I just wanted to say it publicly. I speak of my drummer and this is his last show tonight. He's twenty years old and his name is Ricky Porrello. I'd like you to help me say goodbye to him. A big one. (applause) Go ahead babe. Do it.

(shaking head) Twenty years old. (laughter) He can have seventy careers.

Sammy Davis Jr. – Harrah's, Lake Tahoe, Nevada. July, 1983

Rick Porrello wears many hats. He is a veteran police lieutenant, jazz drummer, website host, and author. Rick's first book grew out of his research into the murders of his grandfather and several uncles, all of whom were Prohibition-era mob leaders. The result was regional best seller *The Rise and Fall of the Cleveland Mafia – Corn Sugar and Blood* (Barricade Books, 1995). Rick followed that book with *To Kill the Irishman – The War that Crippled the Mafia* (Next Hat Press, 1998), which is the story of Danny Greene, a notorious Irish-American racketeer whose murder proved instrumental in the fall of several Mafia families. To Kill the Irishman remains under option for a motion picture.

When he isn't fighting crime or writing about it, Rick can usually be found perfecting his technique on a set of drums. An accomplished jazz drummer, he began his greatest musical achievement in 1981, at age eighteen, when he took over the drum throne from his brother Ray Porrello, then stickman for Sammy Davis, Jr. That fortunate break started Rick on a two-and-a-half year stint involving extensive worldwide travel to Europe, South America, Australia, Mexico, and of course the regular U.S. "Rat Pack" venues of Las Vegas, Reno, Lake Tahoe, and Atlantic City. Accompanying Sammy Davis, Jr., Rick also had the honor of working with the great Count Basie and has appeared on television several times, including on the Tonight Show starring Johnny Carson.

Despite the excitement and promise of such early success with the drums, a second career interest eventually pulled Rick from the Sammy Davis, Jr. gig, and he returned to Cleveland to begin college studies. In 1986, despite opposition from family and friends, Rick traded his drumsticks for a badge and .38 special when he joined a Cleveland-area police department. Since childhood he has had an increasing interest in police work, and despite a skyrocketing music career, he decided that protecting the public was more important to him than entertaining them.

When his duties as a police officer allow, Rick continues to perform regionally and he hosts the popular organized crime website, *AmericanMafia.com*. He is married with two children and lives in suburban Cleveland.